Artillery in Color
1920–1963

ARTILLERY
IN COLOR
1920–1963

by

IAN HOGG

illustrated by
PETER SARSON *and* TONY BRYAN

ARCO PUBLISHING, INC.
NEW YORK

Published by Arco Publishing, Inc.
219 Park Avenue South, New York, N.Y. 10003

Copyright © 1980 by Ian Hogg

Printed in Great Britain

Library of Congress Cataloging in Publication Data

Hogg, Ian V 1926–
  Artillery in color, 1920–1963.
  Includes index.
  1. Ordnance. I. Sarson, Peter, joint author.
  II. Bryan, Tony, joint author. III. Title.
  UF520.H62   358'.1   80–379
  ISBN 0–668–04939–1 (Cloth Edition)
  ISBN 0–668–04941–3 (Paper Edition)

CONTENTS

THE POSTWAR YEARS

When the reverberations of World War I died away in 1919, the combatants could look back on a war which had been predominantly an artillery battle, a circumstance which had come about simply because the war had turned into a gigantic siege. Since sieges were always reduced by artillery fire before the foot-soldiers made their assault, all the combatants stocked up with heavy artillery. So that when the war was over, they all had full artillery parks and enough equipment to last them for many years; all, that is, except Germany who was stripped of most of her equipment under the terms of the Versailles Treaty, forbidden to have anti-tank or anti-aircraft guns in the field armies, forbidden tanks, and with her gun-makers severely restricted in what they could build for export.

Nevertheless, for all that they were well-stocked with equipment, most of the world's artillerymen were conscious that much of it was obsolescent. The greater part of the equipment used in 1914–18 had actually been designed well before the war; in most cases modifications had been made during the course of the war to achieve greater range or better mobility, but essentially the guns were old and if one assumed that there would be a few years of peace before the next war came along, then by that time they would be quite out of date. It followed, then, that the design and development of artillery ought to be put in hand. The employment of artillery, too, was a field which had to be closely examined.

The advent of the tank and the aeroplane, the increasing use of mechanical transport, improvements in methods of communication, the possibility of observing the effects of artillery fire from an aircraft, all these things had appeared during the war; some had been tried in a hurried manner, some had had to be put to one side, but there was now time to examine them and see how they would all fit into the postwar armies. The fact that the late war was currently being spoken of as 'the war to end wars' cut little ice with the soldiers; they generally had a less sanguine view of human nature than did the politicians.

The principal artillery technique of the 1914–18 war had been to saturate the enemy areas with a drumfire of shells sometimes lasting for days, the intention being to break down wire obstacles, smash trenches and render the enemy troops incapable of manning or using their weapons. In many respects this system failed; the tens of thousands of shells ripped up the ground and made it almost impassable for the assaulting troops, while the enemy soon learned to build deep shelters to protect him during the bombardment and from which he could emerge with his machine-guns when the shelling stopped and before the assaulting infantry reached him. Attempts to close this gap by keeping the infantry closer to the barrage of shells did not always succeed; the French, for example, laid down that unless the infantry suffered some 10 to 15 per cent casualties from their own artillery, they were not following their barrage close enough. Needless to say, this was not a policy which was calculated to endear the artillery to the remainder of the army.

Postwar examination of this type of artillery employment led to a realization that much of the trouble stemmed from the inability to communicate from the front line to the guns. When the battle situation changed, it was impossible to reach the artillery and tell them to make some suitable alteration in their fire, and so it was necessary to produce relatively rigid plans of bombardment and barrage and set them in motion, hoping that they would be largely successful. If communication, from forward observers to the gun batteries, could be perfected, it would no longer be necessary to prepare rigid set-piece plans and the fire of the artillery could be directed to those areas where it would do most good.

Another problem was the question of moving the guns to take advantage of success. Frequently, in France, the Allies had put in an attack, the infantry had captured their objectives, they had pushed on, and then, at a critical moment, they had gone beyond the effective protection of their own artillery, to be exposed to fire from the other side's guns. The extensive shelling of the battlefield had effectively barred the way for the accompanying artillery, since it could not, with horse teams or ponderous caterpillar tractors, make its way through the morass of shell holes to take up new positions. This came down to a twofold question, firstly in relation to the previous one of excessive bombardment on cast-iron plans, and secondly to the matter of bestowing better mobility on the guns.

By the same token, if the guns could be improved to give more range, then their effective covering power would be increased and the infantry would have that much more protection in their advance, and this consideration reinforced the arguments that the guns of 1919 were at the final stages of their development, little more could be extracted from them, and therefore new designs had to be initiated. But the question of what sort of guns had to be designed was intimately tied in with the question of what sort of employment was envisaged.

Leaving aside such specialized machines as the Paris Gun and the enormous 42 cm 'Big Bertha' howitzers used to reduce the Belgian forts in 1914, the artillery of the 1914–18 period fell into certain broad groups and showed striking similarities between nations. First came the divisional field gun; this was of 3 inch (76 mm) calibre in the British Army, 75 mm in the French, 77 mm in the German and Austrian,

3 inch in the Russian and 75 mm in the American armies. All fired a shell of 15–18 lbs weight and all had been primarily designed to fire a shrapnel shell since at the time of their inception, about the turn of the century, shrapnel was the prime man-killing projectile for use against troops in the open. The shrapnel shell consisted of a hollow shell body filled with lead balls and a small gunpowder expelling charge; fitted with a time fuze it was arranged to burst in the air slightly short of its intended target so that the gunpowder charge blew the balls from the shell body in a cone. Given velocity by the forward motion of the shell, these bullets then scythed down through the ranks of the troops at the target. It will be appreciated, though, that a shrapnel shell could do little or no damage to *matériel*, and during the war years the high explosive shell came into increasing use in order to solve the problems which arose when the troops began to vanish into trenches and dugouts. But a 75 mm or 3 inch gun high explosive shell, particularly of wartime manufacture, was insufficiently powerful to have any serious effect on entrenchments or pillboxes except when fired in overwhelming numbers.

To make a serious impression with a high explosive shell, it was necessary to move up to the next category, the medium guns and howitzers. The British had a highly effective 4.5 inch (114 mm) and the Germans a 105 mm (4.1 inch) howitzer, and these were extensively used to back up the fire of the field guns and provide more destructive power. The French were never able to persuade their purse-holders of the utility of a light howitzer and never had a comparable weapon, a defect they were determined to remedy. Their prime reliance was placed in a 155 mm (6.1 inch) howitzer, a weapon also adopted by the American Army upon their entrance into the war.

Howitzers are characterized by short barrels and multiple charge systems which allow the gunner a number of trajectory options, all of which describe an arc high in the sky so as to pass the shell over intervening obstacles. Since so much of the propellant's energy is expended in throwing the shell high into the air, the resulting range is relatively short. In order to reach farther into enemy territory the gun is used; this fires at a flatter trajectory, uses, generally, a somewhat lighter shell and heavier charge, attains a greater velocity, and thus sends the shell much farther. Medium guns thus formed the basic means of long-range fire from well behind the line in order to silence enemy batteries, and the French used a 155 mm weapon of considerable power, again a design taken into service by the American Army. Britain had their 5 inch (127 mm) 'sixty-pounder' gun, a number of six inch (152 mm) guns, and a small number of elderly 4.7 inch (120 mm) guns. Germany relied principally on a 150 mm (5.9 inch) weapon, as did Austria, while the Russians used a 152 mm very similar to the British weapon.

In the very highest calibres howitzers, for great destructive power, were common; Britain used a 9.2 inch (233 mm), 12 inch (305 mm) and a few 15 inch (380 mm) weapons, Germany 21 cm (8.2 inch) and 24 cm (9.45 inch), France 21 cm and 24 cm weapons. At this level of equipment, the transportation problem became a serious one, and these weapons had to be laboriously dismantled into several units for transport behind either horse teams or tractors, and then laboriously put together at their firing sites, a procedure adequate for the siege conditions of the war but far from satisfactory when the war entered a fluid stage. For similar reasons, the very largest weapons – British 9.2 inch and 12 inch guns, French 34 cm and 40 cm guns, German 28 cm and 30 cm guns, were railway mounted so that they could be moved with moderate rapidity wherever railway tracks could be laid.

This array of weapons continued into the postwar period, but it can be seen that, except for some of the smaller guns and howitzers, little of it was suited to a war of movement. Moreover there was still this urge to produce weapons of equal convenience of movement as the smaller guns but with greater range and greater destructive power.

Probably the first country to make a thorough study of the artillery's employment and equipment during the war was America. On 11 December 1918 the US War Department convened a Board of Officers 'to make a study of the armament, calibers and types of *matériel*, kinds and proportions of ammunition, and methods of transport of the artillery to be assigned to a Field Army.' From the name of its presiding officer, Brig-General William I. Westervelt, this Board went down in history as the 'Westervelt Board', sometimes called the 'Caliber Board' and its recommendations, which it produced on 23 May 1919, formed the basis of American artillery development for several years; indeed, some of its effects can still be seen in American equipment to this day.

The American Army was particularly interested in the question of providing artillery equipment, since it had been badly caught out in 1917. Its in-service designs were obsolete by European standards, while various designs then under development turned out to need much more development and modification before they would be ready for adoption. They therefore were forced to purchase equipment from abroad; British 8 inch howitzers and 6 inch guns, French 75 mm field guns and 155 mm howitzers and guns were adopted and the designs were put out to tender for manufacture in the USA. Since few American firms had any experience in the manufacture of artillery, progress was slow and only a handful of US-made guns and howitzers were ready when the war ended. In addition to this production problem, there was the nagging doubt that the selected weapons might not necessarily be the best ones, and hence the Westervelt Board examined all the various types of artillery which had been used by every nation during the war before reaching its conclusions.

The types recommended by the Westervelt Board were firstly a light field gun in the 75 mm class, accompanied by a field howitzer of about 105 mm calibre; second, a medium field howitzer of 155 mm calibre; third, a heavy field gun of 155 mm calibre; and lastly a heavy howitzer of about 9.5 inch calibre. They then recommended research into the shape and design of projectiles to attain the best possible range and destructive power, the development of motor traction and self-propelled guns on tracked carriages, a 3 inch and a 4.7 inch anti-aircraft gun, and the provision of railway guns as both heavy siege artillery and also as movable coast defence weapons. It was an ambitious programme, calculated to keep the Ordnance Department hard at work for several years.

In Britain and France the post-mortem was less formal, but it took place in much the same fashion, and the results were perhaps less clear-cut. The British 18 pounder (3.3 inch or 84 mm) and 4.5 inch howitzer were both at more or less the end of their possible development, having both been improved during the war, and the expressed opinion was that a single weapon should be developed to replace them, something with a better range than the 18 pounder and a more destructive shell than the 4.5 inch. The French were still convinced that their 75 mm gun, which had entered service amid clouds of secrecy in 1897, was still a formidable weapon which made up for its light shell by its high rate of fire; it could, therefore, remain in service but it needed to be accompanied by a field howitzer.

During the 1920s the reaction against the recent carnage set in and in every nation the military forces were reduced in men and equipment and given very little money with which to pursue development; and of what money was available, a large proportion of it went into the development of aircraft and tanks, those two mechanical wonders which had come to fruition in 1914–18. What was available for other military needs was often earmarked for various strategic schemes; thus in France the greater part of the military budget went into the ground in the construction of the Maginot Line,

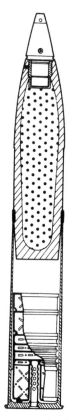
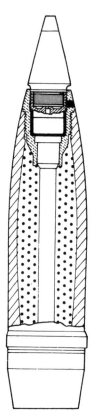

Complete round for the American 105 mm howitzer, with high explosive shell, impact fuze and multi-part charge in the cartridge case.

An American white phosphorus smoke shell. The central burster carries just enough explosive to break open the shell on impact and release the phosphorus to form a smoke cloud.

while Britain devoted most of her funds to developing coast defence weapons and equipment for the future Fortress of Singapore. But sufficient managed to trickle through for some progress to be made, and in default of actual manufactured guns the various theoretical proposals could be examined, refined, criticized, re-refined, re-examined and hammered out to the last bolt and rivet at very little cost, culminating in a set of drawings which could then be put to one side until finance was forthcoming, or torn up in favour of starting again with a clean sheet of paper.

By about 1930 some sort of order can be discerned in all the various reports of activity. The American Army had developed a useful 105 mm howitzer, had perfected a 240 mm heavy howitzer which they had bought from France but virtually had to redesign before it worked properly, had standardized the wartime French 155 mm gun and howitzer but were working on improved designs, and had prototype models of useful 3 inch and 105 mm anti-aircraft guns.

Britain was still debating the merits of various types of field gun or howitzer, had produced a small number of a very good self-propelled gun to work with the Experimental Armoured Force, and had drawn up specifications for its future anti-aircraft gun. It had also designed a 15 inch coast gun for use in Singapore and an unusual twin-barrelled 6 pounder (57 mm) fast-firing coast defence gun for repelling motor torpedo-boats from defended harbours.

The French had, as might be expected, put most of their development effort into special artillery to be mounted in the fortresses of the Maginot Line, but they had also found time to develop some anti-aircraft guns and were working, at last, on a 105 mm field howitzer to supplement their 75 mm guns.

In Germany things were progressing in a devious fashion. The Allied Disarmament Commission were able to ensure that no warlike stores were produced in the principal gun-making factories, but they were, of course, quite unable to oversee what was going on in design offices and behind closed doors. A 105 mm field howitzer had been designed and the drawings filed away, while an oblique approach to re-armament was demonstrated by the development of a portable turntable which could be rapidly laid down and used to position railway guns so that they could fire in any direction. The development and training of anti-aircraft batteries is an interesting example of how the Treaty provisions were sidetracked in this period. At the end of 1919 the only AA guns left to the Germans were some permanently-mounted guns in the Fortress of Königsberg and those on ships of the German Navy. But a number of AA guns escaped scrapping and were 'converted' into 'field guns' by simply removing the specialized AA sights and placing a block on the elevating gear so that the gun could not be brought to bear on high-flying targets. These were then issued as the armament of seven motorized batteries, one of which was attached to each of the seven artillery regiments permitted to the reduced German Army. This was then dormant until 1925 when the officers of these batteries were attached to the German Navy for several months, supposedly as liaison officers but actually to be trained in anti-aircraft gunnery, using the navy's guns. In 1928 the converted batteries were quietly re-equipped with new 75 mm guns, built by Krupp ostensibly for export but then, by various middlemen and 'front' companies, shuffled back and forth until they vanished from sight, to re-appear in the wastes of East Prussia, whither the motorized batteries were sent for training. The converted field guns were re-converted back into their original role, and by 1930 the German Army had the makings of an anti-aircraft force, probably a stronger one than any other country had at that time.

But for the accession of Adolf Hitler to power in 1933, and the subsequent rise of Nazi Germany, doubtless the western nations would have continued their desultory experimenting with various types of artillery without getting very much done. As it was, 1933 can be seen to mark the turning point between rather dilettante pottering among the designs and single-minded pursuit of specific aims. In Britain the decision was finally taken to go for a gun–howitzer firing a 25 lb shell to a range of, if possible, 15,000 yards, and in the following year a design of 3.7 inch AA gun to fire a 28 lb shell to a ceiling of 28,000 feet was approved. The French finally agreed on a design of 105 mm howitzer and arranged for production to begin in 1935. The Americans had been pitch-forked into mechanization by General MacArthur and as a result were busily re-working their 105 mm howitzer into a model capable of high-speed towing behind a motor truck. They were also working on new types of 155 mm gun and 8 inch howitzer, more powerful than the wartime models and on new split-trail carriages which permitted higher elevations and thus more flexible tactical use. But the distance between Germany and the USA was such that the Americans could raise little enthusiasm or money for the pursuit of their new designs and they were thus having to proceed very slowly.

A new category of weapon which was being studied at this time was the anti-tank gun. The first purpose-built anti-tank weapon had been a heavy single-shot rifle of 13 mm calibre developed by Mauser and issued to German troops in 1918. This was still a viable method of attack, relative to the thinly-armoured tanks of the day, but it was a simple one-man weapon and whilst it could make life unpleasant for the occupants of the tank it was unlikely to be able to stop one without a great deal of luck. What was required was a small-calibre high-velocity cannon which would project a hard-ened shell containing a small charge of high explosive and a base fuze; this would penetrate the armour of the tank and, once inside, detonate to inflict injuries on the crew and severe, disabling, damage to the tank itself. During World War 1 the Germans had developed a light automatic gun of 20 mm calibre for use by aircraft; after the war the rights to this were bought by a Swiss company and it was marketed as the Oerlikon gun, largely as a light anti-aircraft weapon but also as a potential small-calibre infantry support and anti-tank gun. Most nations tried them out, but felt that the shell was a little too small to be really effective, bearing in mind the possibility that tanks might begin wearing thicker armour in the future. Therefore the consensus of opinion seemed to settle around the 37–40 mm calibre, a size which promised an effective projectile fired by a gun light enough to be man-handled into place by three or four men and easily concealed in an ambush position.

Anti-aircraft artillery was the other field of great technical interest in the early 1930s. There were, apparently, two methods of approach to the problem of shooting down air-craft. One was to develop a medium or heavy calibre gun which fired a shell capable of downing any existing aircraft with a single shot. This, unfortunately, demanded an extremely high degree of accuracy in aiming so as to fetch aircraft and shell together in the same place at the same time, and the technical problems involved in such accurate fire control were formidable. The other approach was to adopt a light, fast-firing gun which could emit a stream of shells and fill the sky with metal, in the hope that one of the shells or some of the splinters might fall into the path of the aircraft and thus damage it. This light gun could then be directed upwards by eye and 'hose-piped' about until it achieved success. The foremost development in this field was a 40 mm weapon developed by the Swedish firm of AB Bofors; it was mounted on a light four-wheeled carriage and fired a two-pound (1 kg) shell from four-round clips at a rate of 120 shots a minute. The shell was fitted with a tracer unit which burned and emitted a red light which outlined the shell's flight through the air, thus giving the gunlayer a visual indication of his accuracy, and at the end of a few seconds flight the tracer lit a self-destruction charge which exploded the shell in the air, so that it did not come down to earth live and primed ready to explode on contact.

In the larger anti-aircraft gun field, 1933 was a significant year because it saw the introduction of a gun which was to become a legend in its own lifetime: the German 88 mm Flak 18. This gun had its beginnings in 1925 when the German Army came to the conclusion that 75 mm was not a large enough calibre and Krupp were asked to develop something more powerful. At that time the restrictions of the Versailles Treaty had left the German gunmaking industry in something of a decline, and Krupp had sent some of their designers abroad to work with other companies. One such team had gone to AB Bofors in Sweden and, when not working for Bofors' benefit, they had designed an 88 mm gun firing a 20 lb (9.1 kg) shell. In 1931 they returned to Germany with the drawings; prototypes were built and tested, the Army approved, and in 1933 it was put into production. It was a straight-forward design of high-velocity gun with an ingenious semi-automatic breech mechanism, mounted on a cruciform platform with outriggers. On the move, two two-wheeled limbers attached to the fixed outriggers while the other two were folded alongside the gun; to bring it into action the carriage was lowered from the limbers by jacks, the outriggers spread, the central pedestal levelled, and the gun was ready for firing at a rate of about fifteen rounds a minute.

1933 also saw the perfecting of the specification for America's basic field gun; their 105 mm howitzer had been developed as a horse-drawn weapon, and it was now called in for re-designing for high-speed traction behind a motor vehicle. In the anti-aircraft field a 105 mm gun, which had been under development since 1924, was finally standardized as a static-mounted weapon for defence of harbours and other defended areas, while designs were also being prepared for improvements to the standard medium and heavy field guns and howitzers.

PREPARATION FOR WAR

In parallel with the development of weapons went the development of techniques and the organization of artillery to more modern standards. In 1928 the British were using radio-telephony in artillery batteries and were well advanced in the development of mechanical traction. The detection of enemy batteries by techniques first explored in 1914–18 was also being perfected; two methods were used, flash-spotting and sound-ranging. Flash-spotting relied upon the flash from the muzzle of the enemy gun being picked up by observers spread across the front; by cross-observation they were able to obtain quite accurate fixes of guns, even when they were masked by intervening crests, since the flash was often reflected from the clouds above. More reliable, though more complicated, was the technique of sound-ranging in which sensitive microphones were buried in patterns behind the front line. In front of them sat an observer who, when he heard enemy guns fire, would switch on the microphone circuit; this was connected to a pen-recording instrument which traced out a pattern showing the time interval between the sound of the guns striking each microphone, and from this pattern it was possible to plot the position of the guns with considerable accuracy. Not only that, it was also possible to range one's own guns on to the enemy battery by listening to the sound of the bursting shells and adjusting the fire until the shell-burst gave an identical pattern to the sound of the enemy gun, an indication that the two were in the same place.

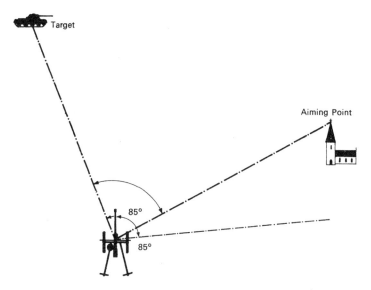

The principle of indirect shooting: the positions of gun, target, and aiming point are plotted on a map and the included angle determined. By setting this angle on the gun's dial sight and pointing the sight at the aiming point, the gun barrel is then pointed at the target.

Such techniques relied upon locating the enemy gun on an arbitrary geographical grid system, and in order to bring fire to bear it was then necessary to have one's own guns located on the same system; this led to the setting up of surveying units who, basing their work on the existing national survey information, would extend the grid system to take in the guns and the observers and, by extension, the enemy guns.

Gunners of all countries always asked the designers for more range, so that they could make their presence felt deeper into enemy territory. But a disadvantage of this was that the simple observer on the front line could only see as far as the next ridge, and his zone of observation could rarely extend as far as the guns were capable of shooting. Observation balloons had been used in 1914–18, a system which lifted the observer well into the air and gave him the command of height, but this system was not suited to mobile warfare. The alternative was to use aircraft, but air forces were busy about their own affairs, most of which involved strategic bombing and fighter defence and had little thought for more direct support of armies in the field. In such circumstances, the British began experimenting with the use of light aircraft to observe gunfire, experiments which, at first, were privately conducted by officers who were keen amateur flyers.

* * *

As the war came closer, so the armies settled on their basic weapons. In 1936 the British received the first supplies of their new fieldpiece, though it was something of a compromise. The ideal specification had called for a 3.7 inch (94 mm) gun-howitzer firing a 25 lb (11.3 kg) shell, but financial considerations had ruled the day and the calibre was reduced to 3.45 inches (87 mm), which allowed a barrel to be made which could then be inserted into the jacket of the old 18 pounder field gun, accept the breech mechanism of the 18 pounder, and thus produce a new gun on an old carriage. While this was an adequate stopgap, the 18 pounder carriage could not take the full force of the ammunition designed to go with the gun, and thus the combination was restricted to a maximum range of 12,800 yards (11,700 m) instead of the 15,000 yards (13,700 m) the designers had been told to achieve. So while the '18/25-pounder' (an unofficial but fully descriptive name) was issued, designers went ahead with a completely new carriage which would allow the full potential of the gun to be realized.

Early in 1938 the new 25 pounder carriages appeared, two prototypes, both with split trails and both, in the eyes of their future users, far too cumbersome to be practical. In order to produce an alternative carriage for comparative trials, an

The Auster 6 Air Observation Post, the 'Eye in the Sky' which gave wartime artillery a vastly enhanced sphere of observation and effect.

elderly Vickers model, with box trail and with a round firing platform beneath it, was hurriedly adapted to the new gun, and all three prototypes sent to the School of Artillery for testing. The tests took no more than a day, and on a show of hands from the various artillerymen who had observed the tests, the box-trail design was selected for manufacture. In this somewhat haphazard manner, the eventual form of the British 25 pounder gun was arrived at, and events were to prove the rightness of the decision.

The German equivalent of the 25 pounder was the 105 mm Light Field Howitzer Model 18. This had been originally designed in 1929/30 by the Rheinmetall company, at a time when the German Army were earnestly debating whether to adopt 75 mm as their standard divisional gun calibre or go to 105 mm in order to benefit from the heavier shell. Eventually, due to the more generous financial climate of German re-armament, they were able to do both, retaining the 75 mm calibre but also adopting the 105 mm howitzer, and in 1935 the Model 18 was formally introduced into service. It was mounted on a split-trail carriage and had the recoil system components split into two; the recoil buffer was inside the cradle, under the gun, while the hydro-pneumatic recuperator cylinder was mounted above the barrel where it could easily dissipate its heat. It was a good, workmanlike, design, if somewhat heavy, and fired a 14.8 kg (32.6 lb) shell to 10,675 m (11,675 yards). Since the German artillery was still largely horse-drawn, the carriage used wooden-spoked, steel-tyred wheels; later, when motor traction became more frequent, pressed-steel spoked wheels with solid rubber tyres were adopted.

The French Army still placed their faith in their 75 mm M1897 gun, with its rapid-fire capability, though in truth it was obsolescent by the 1930s. In an endeavour to improve matters, the 'Mle 97/33' appeared in 1933, the same gun but on a new split-trail carriage which allowed more elevation and thus more range. It was a poor design, however, and the

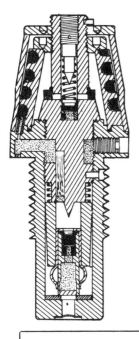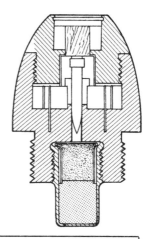

Typical fuzes: on the left, a French time fuze which relied on a coil of lead tube containing gunpowder for its timing system. The tube was pierced at a pre-determined point; on firing, the central firing pin set back, struck the detonator beneath and ignited the gunpowder train which burned to the desired time and then fired the charge at the bottom of the fuze. If the time was set too long and the fuze struck the ground, then the unit at the bottom would fly forward, the detonator would strike the fixed needle, and the shell would be initiated.

On the right, an 'Aufschlagzunder 38' German nose fuze used with hollow charge shell. Hinged blocks keep the firing pin away from the detonator until they are swung aside by the spinning of the shell, leaving the pin free to be driven down when the fuze strikes the target.

Army rapidly disposed of them, selling most of them to Brazil. More important, though, was the French Army's realization that something with a heavier weight of shell was needed to back up the 75 mm guns, and in 1934 a 105 mm howitzer was adopted. The first model, the 'Mle 34S' was developed by Schneider and was a conventional split-trail design with a performance close to that of the German 105 mm. Schneider could not produce these fast enough, and so the state arsenal at Bourges was asked to produce a similar weapon, which became the 'Mle 35B'. This had a shorter barrel and thus slightly less range, but used an interesting split-trail carriage in which the large pressed-steel wheels were attached to the trail legs in such a way that as the legs were swung open, so the wheels moved to form a shield for the gunners.

The Italian Army were equipped with a varied collection of ordnance, most of which was of elderly design. Among the most numerous was the 75 mm 'Modello 11', a gun with some remarkable features; as the name implies it had been developed in 1911 by an engineer called Deport and was the first service artillery piece anywhere in the world to use the split trail type of carriage. Needless to say, this innovation was closely studied by others, and the split trail was widely copied in future years. Another oddity of the Modello 11 was the recoil system; the cylinders and pistons were in the usual place, inside a rectangular cradle beneath the barrel, but when the barrel was elevated the cradle stayed where it was, together with the recoil system. The barrel was trunnioned about an adapter unit at the rear of the cradle which connected it to the recoil pistons; just what sort of compound forces this arrangement must have set up can be imagined, but in spite of all the theoretical objections – and there are many – it worked, and continued to work, so well that Modello 11 guns stayed in use throughout the 1939–45 war.

In the 1930s the Italians, as with others, came to the conclusion that a heavier projectile would be of assistance, and in

1939 the 'Obice da 105/14' appeared; 'Obice' means howitzer, and the notation '105/14', as with all Italian artillery, indicates the calibre of the gun and also the length of the barrel expressed in multiples of the calibre. In this case, the barrel was 14 calibres long, i.e. 14×105 mm or 1470 mm. The 105/14 was developed by the Ansaldo company and was a somewhat cumbersome design with a relatively poor performance; its maximum range was but 8,160 m, in comparison with the 10,675 m of the German 105 mm and 11,160 for the American. Its introduction was late and the relatively poor Italian industrial capacity was incapable of providing the numbers necessary to fully re-equip the army so that the majority of Italian divisional support units had to rely upon the 75 mm weapons.

The Japanese had been involved in warfare in Manchuria since 1930, but the form of warfare in that area involved little use of artillery and they therefore had small incentive to innovation. For the most part they relied upon a variety of 75 mm weapons, most of which had been introduced into service between the Russo-Japanese War and World War I and which were either European-built or Japanese-built under licence from the original manufacturers, Schneider or Krupp. Their principal field piece was the 75 mm 'Type 38 Improved', a weapon which introduces us to several features of Japanese artillery in one package. Firstly, the nomenclature: 'Type 38' (sometimes rendered as '38th Year') indicates that it was introduced into service in the 38th year of the current Emperor's reign, in this case the reign of the Emperor Mutsuhutu which was known as the 'Meiji Era', from 1868 to 1911. Thus the 38th Year becomes 1905. The system was continued into the 'Taisho Era' from 1912–25 (Emperor Yoshihito) and the 'Showa Era' which began under Emperor Hirohito in 1926. A moment's thought will show that there was then a danger of having two toally different weapons with the same Type number, since both 1912 and 1926 could be Year One. This was avoided at first by referring to 'Taisho

1' or 'Showa 1' but this got too involved, and in 1928 the system was changed. Henceforth all Japanese equipment introduced into service was given a model number tied to the year in the Japanese calendar; this differs from the Christian calendar by 660 years, so that a weapon introduced in 1935 took the Japanese year 2595 and was known as 'Type 95'.

The Type 38 field gun was a Krupp design and fairly conventional for its period. During 1914–18 these weapons were withdrawn to Osaka Arsenal and rebuilt with a new trail which allowed more elevation and thus better range; other mechanical improvements were made and thus it became the 'Type 38 Improved'. Like most Japanese weapons its ratio of weight to range was quite remarkable; for an all-up weight of 1135 kg (2500 lbs) it fired a 6 kg (13.2 lb) shell to 11,970 m (13,080 yards). By comparison, the Krupp 1916 77 mm gun weighed 1325 kg (2920 lbs) and fired a 7 kg (15 lb) shell to 9,100 m (9,950 yds). This combination of light weight and long range appears to have been achieved by accepting a somewhat lower factor of safety than was considered normal in the west, but it seems to have worked well enough.

But even if the Type 38 Improved was good enough for warlords in Manchuria, the Japanese General Staff were astute enough to realize that something better would be required if and when they ventured farther afield, and in 1930 the 75 mm Type 90 gun was introduced in considerable secrecy. The secrecy was partly due to the usual military desire for concealment of new weapons, and also to the fact that the design had been filched from Schneider of France, the Type 90 being almost a perfect copy of Schneider's 85 mm M1927 which they had supplied to the Greek Army. From its specification the Type 90 appeared to be an excellent weapon; it used a modern split trail carriage with either wooden or pneumatic wheels, had a long barrel with muzzle brake, and with a weight of 1400 kg (3085 lbs) ranged to 15,000 m (16,400 yards). Unfortunately it failed to live up to its promise; few were built, they were issued to the Manchurian Army, and they were later withdrawn. The trouble appears to have been in the recoil system, a complicated mechanism requiring careful maintenance and cossetting, which it was unlikely to receive in Manchuria in the late 1930s.

WAR

The first few months of war, in 1939 and 1940, were of use to artillery formations of all the armies involved in so far as they permitted peacetime theories to be put to the test of war in a relatively gentle manner, and in this period there were minor re-adjustments and re-organizations. But the eruption of the German invasion of France and the Low Countries in 1940 placed more stress on the units involved and began to show some of the defects. The British field artillery, for example, had been extensively re-organized in 1938, each field regiment of 24 guns being split into two 12-gun batteries each of three four-gun troops. The basic flaw in this system, which had been foisted on to the gunners from above, was that the field regiment was intended to support the infantry brigade and the brigade contained three infantry battalions; two batteries could not be divided between three battalions without severe dislocation of the administrative and fire control system, and the fluid actions in France soon made this obvious. As a result, the regiment was re-structured; it retained the same number of guns but was now to be divided into three 8-gun batteries of two four-gun troops each.

An equipment defect which made itself apparent to both sides was that the current anti-tank guns were marginal in their performance and it would not be long before the improvements in tanks would leave them behind. The British 2 pounder of 40 mm and the German 37 mm gun both found themselves hard put to it to penetrate enemy tanks

GERMAN FIELD ARTILLERY BATTERY 1940

Three of these batteries, plus a medium battery of four 15 cm howitzers and four 105 mm guns, formed the artillery regiment of an artillery division.

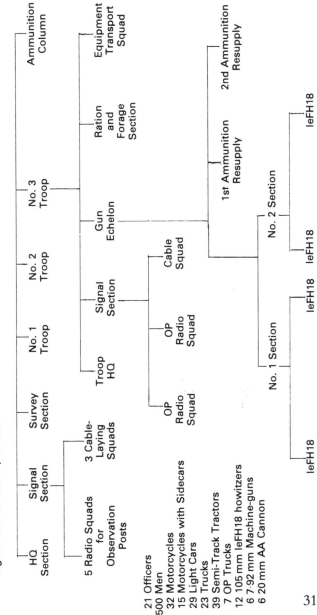

21 Officers
500 Men
32 Motorcycles
15 Motorcycles with Sidecars
29 Light Cars
23 Trucks
39 Semi-Track Tractors
7 OP Trucks
12 105 mm leFH18 howitzers
6 7·92 mm Machine-guns
6 20 mm AA Cannon

except at suicidally short ranges and in both armies the call was for a heavier weapon. The Germans had been working on a 50 mm gun since 1938 and by the end of 1940 they had put it into production. The British had also, in 1938, developed an improved gun of 57 mm calibre, known, in the usual British manner, as the 'six pounder'. Now was the time to bring it into service, but other considerations now came to the fore. The retreat in France and the evacuation from Dunkirk had seen most of the British army's equipment left behind, and among this were no less than 509 2 pounder anti-tank guns. With a German invasion of Britain expected hourly, anti-tank defence was obviously of the highest priority; factories were tooled up to produce the 2 pounder and others to produce the ammunition. To have stopped this production, closed the factories down, changed the tooling, and re-started production of the 6 pounder would have deprived the army of any anti-tank guns at all, and so the decision was taken to continue the 2 pounder in production until the army was fully equipped, and only then to change to producing the 6 pounder.

As a result, when the war moved its activities to the Western Desert the British Army was in a difficult position; the 2 pounder fired only a steel piercing shot. Against it were ranged a variety of German tanks, most of which could fire a 50 mm or 75 mm high explosive shell, and to a greater range than that at which the 2 pounder was dangerous. Their chosen tactic therefore became a matter of standing off, out of danger from the 2 pounder, and shelling the anti-tank gun into silence. The only thing which saved the British forces at this time was a combination of aggressive handling of the 2 pounder, clever concealment in ambush, and the adoption of the 25 pounder gun as an extempore anti-tank gun.

The French campaign had been fought with the 18/25 pounder gun, since production of the perfected model did not begin until late in 1939, and the first complete 25 pounders were used in the abortive Norway campaign. They then

1
The British 13 pounder gun, developed as a Royal Horse Artillery weapon in 1904 and still used by them 75 years later in ceremonial salutes.

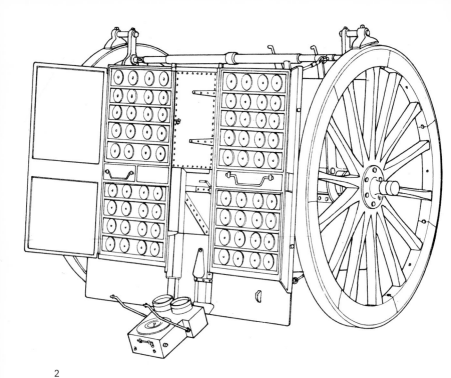

2
The French 75 mm Gun Mle 1897, precursor of all modern artillery,
with its ammunition limber and fuze setter, and, *right*, the operation of
the Nordenfelt Eccentric-Screw Breech mechanism.

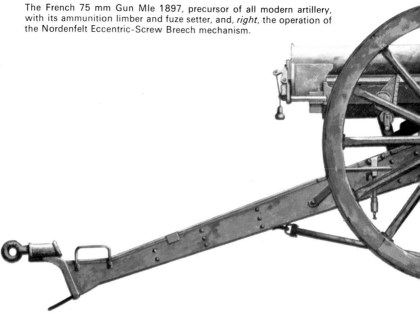

Open

Closed

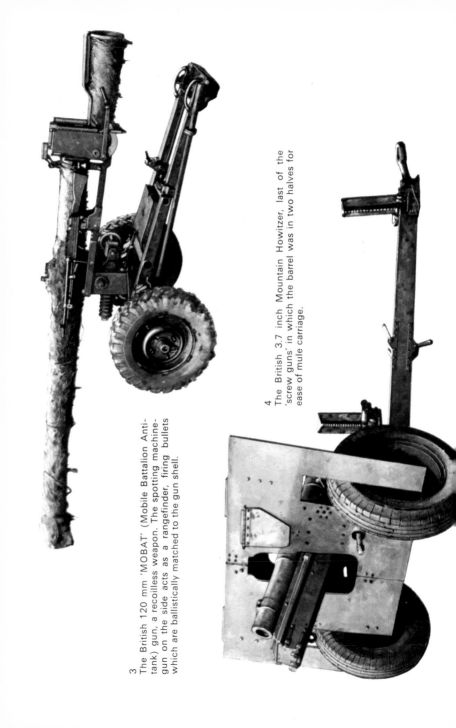

3
The British 120 mm 'MOBAT' (Mobile Battalion Anti-tank) gun, a recoilless weapon. The spotting machine-gun on the side acts as a rangefinder, firing bullets which are ballistically matched to the gun shell.

4
The British 3.7 inch Mountain Howitzer, last of the 'screw guns' in which the barrel was in two halves for ease of mule carriage.

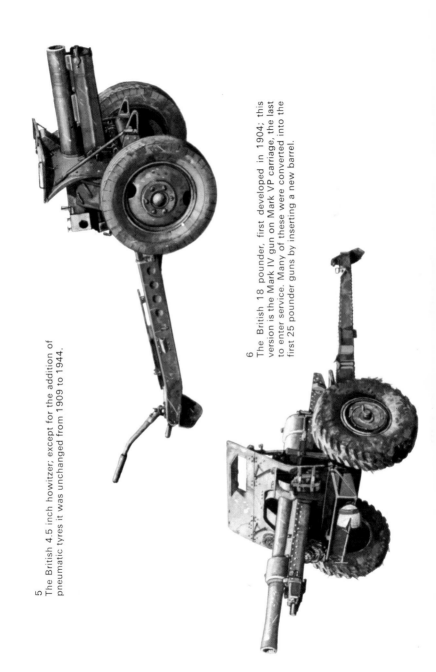

5
The British 4.5 inch howitzer; except for the addition of pneumatic tyres it was unchanged from 1909 to 1944.

6
The British 18 pounder, first developed in 1904; this version is the Mark IV gun on Mark VP carriage, the last to enter service. Many of these were converted into the first 25 pounder guns by inserting a new barrel.

7
The US M 1917 75 mm gun was the British 18 pounder modified to accept French 75 mm ammunition. This version is the M 1917A1, with pneumatic tyres, which appeared in the 1920s.

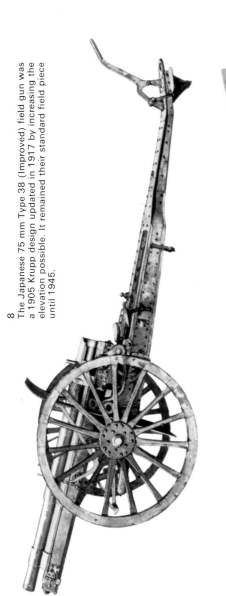

8
The Japanese 75 mm Type 38 (Improved) field gun was a 1905 Krupp design updated in 1917 by increasing the elevation possible. It remained their standard field piece until 1945.

9
The Japanese 70 mm Battalion Howitzer Type 92, a light, short-range weapon which accompanied their infantry and could act as either a direct-fire gun or a high-angle mortar.

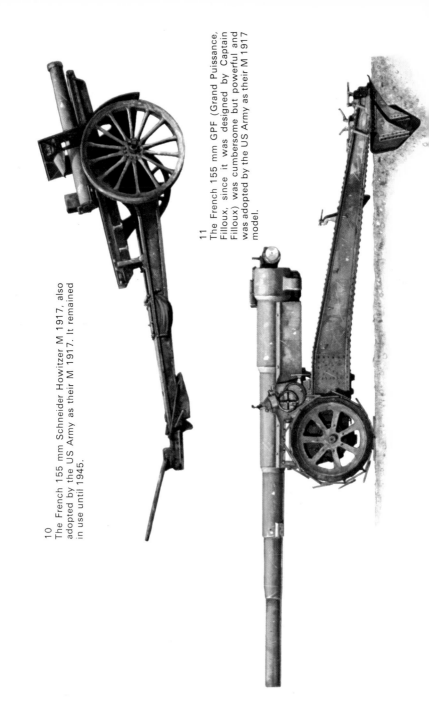

10
The French 155 mm Schneider Howitzer M 1917, also adopted by the US Army as their M 1917. It remained in use until 1945.

11
The French 155 mm GPF (Grand Puissance, Filloux, since it was designed by Captain Filloux) was cumbersome but powerful and was adopted by the US Army as their M 1917 model.

12
The British 9.2 inch Howitzer, developed on the eve of World War I, had to be laboriously dismantled into three loads for transport.

13
Deceptively slender for its five-and-a-half tons, the British 60 pounder medium gun spanned both wars.

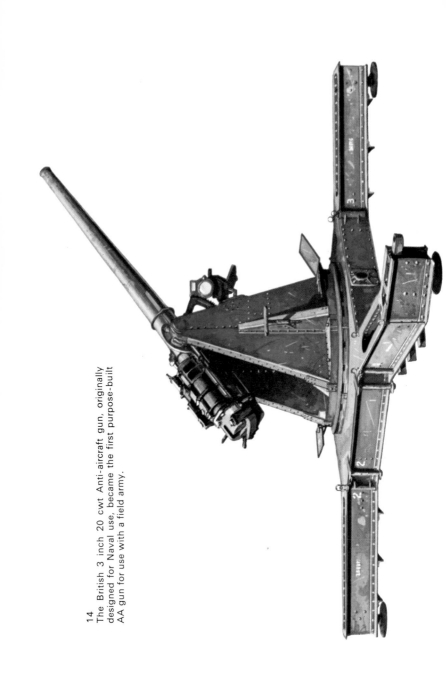

14
The British 3 inch 20 cwt Anti-aircraft gun, originally designed for Naval use, became the first purpose-built AA gun for use with a field army.

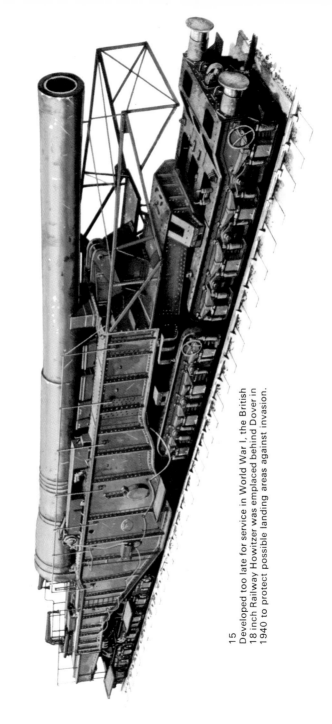

15
Developed too late for service in World War I, the British 18 inch Railway Howitzer was emplaced behind Dover in 1940 to protect possible landing areas against invasion.

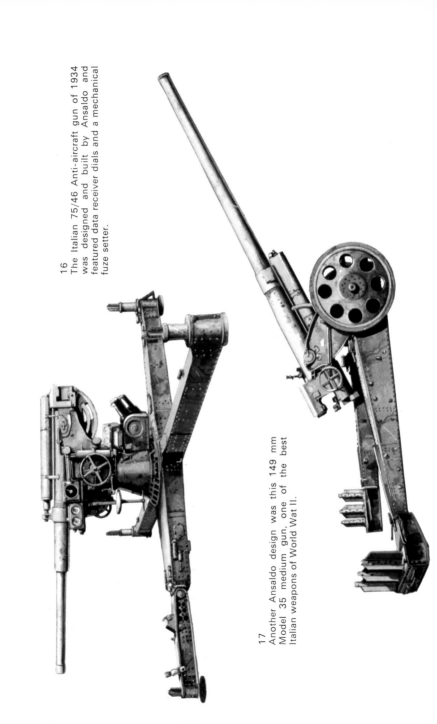

16
The Italian 75/46 Anti-aircraft gun of 1934 was designed and built by Ansaldo and featured data receiver dials and a mechanical fuze setter.

17
Another Ansaldo design was this 149 mm Model 35 medium gun, one of the best Italian weapons of World Wat II.

18
The French 105 mm Mle 1935 field gun had an unusual construction in which the wheels folded inward as the trail legs were opened, so as to provide a shield for the gunners.

19
The French 75 mm Mountain gun Mle 1928 could be dismantled for pack carriage. Many were impressed by the German Army in 1904.

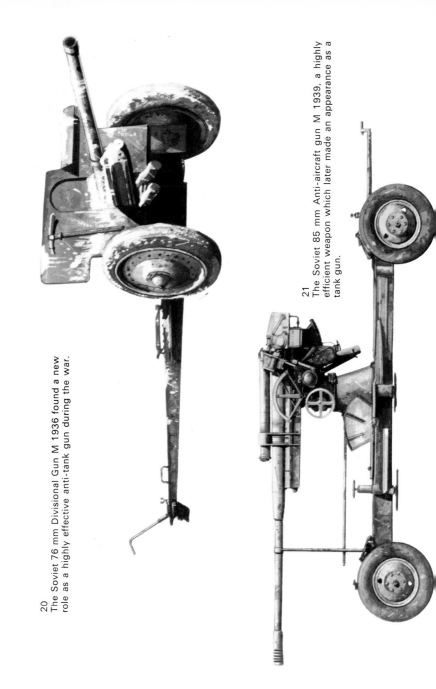

20
The Soviet 76 mm Divisional Gun M 1936 found a new role as a highly effective anti-tank gun during the war.

21
The Soviet 85 mm Anti-aircraft gun M 1939, a highly efficient weapon which later made an appearance as a tank gun.

22
The French Hotchkiss 25 mm M39 Anti-aircraft gun, a great deal of
mounting for not much gun.

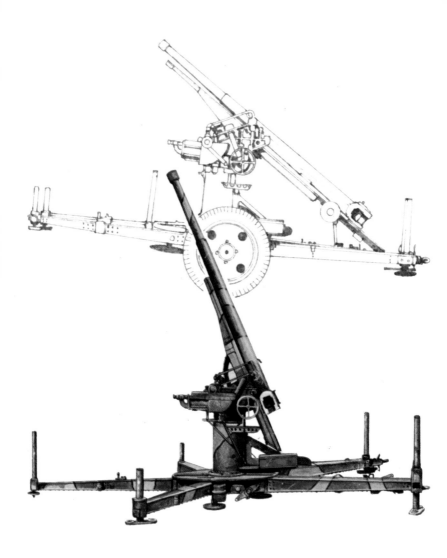

23
The Japanese 75 mm Type 88 Anti-aircraft gun; obsolescent by 1939,
but it formed the mainstay of Jap air defence. The upper drawing
shows the manner in which the barrel was drawn back in the cradle
and locked to the carriage for travelling.

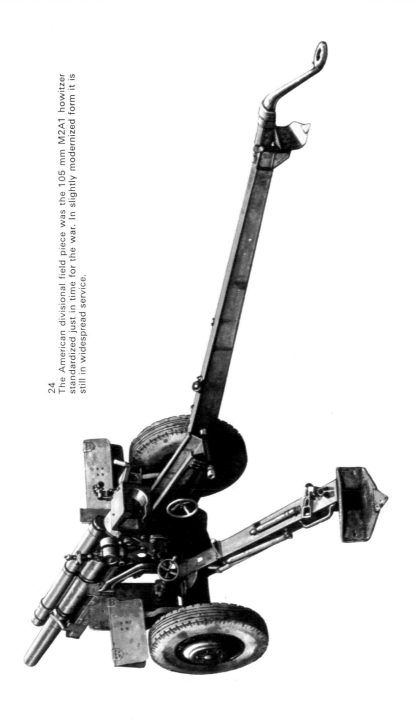

24
The American divisional field piece was the 105 mm M2A1 howitzer standardized just in time for the war. In slightly modernized form it is still in widespread service.

25
Backbone of the German divisional artillery was this 105 mm light field howitzer Model 18. The *inset* drawing shows a typical single-canister smoke shell used for producing smoke screens or, with coloured smoke, for signalling.

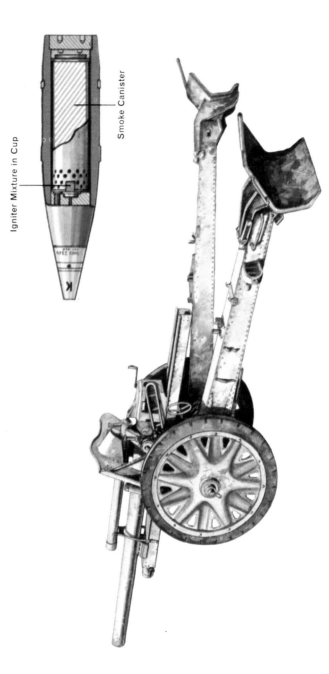

Igniter Mixture in Cup

Smoke Canister

26
The German 7.5 cm infantry gun 18, a light and handy weapon used by infantry heavy weapons companies to give immediate fire support to front line troops.

27
The German 75 mm Feldkanone 38, originally designed by Krupp for the Brazilian Army. The outbreak of war interrupted the contract and the balance were taken by the German Army.

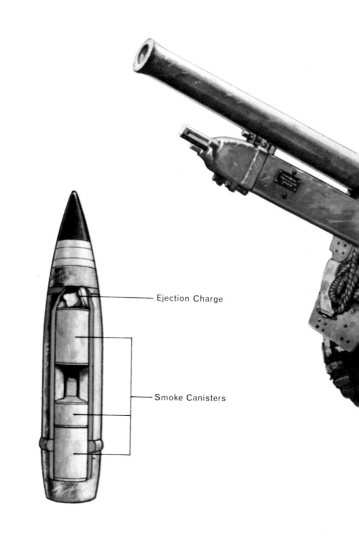

Ejection Charge

Smoke Canisters

28

The British 25 pounder field gun, one of the most versatile weapons of its class. On the *left*, a cut-away view of a smoke shell; *below*, the gun hooked up to its ammunition trailer.

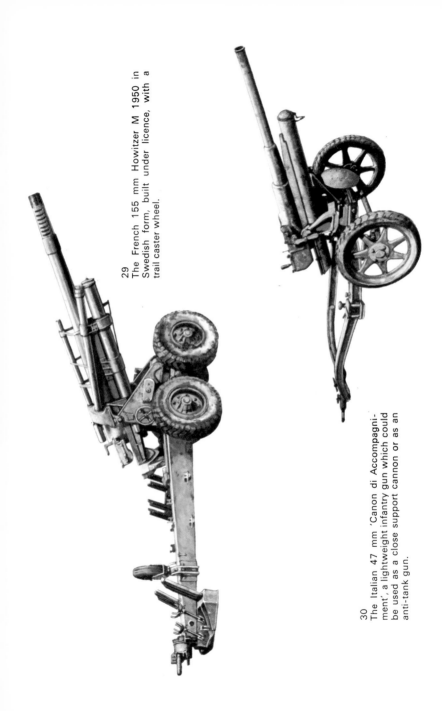

29
The French 155 mm Howitzer M 1950 in Swedish form, built under licence, with a trail caster wheel.

30
The Italian 47 mm 'Canon di Accompagniment', a lightweight infantry gun which could be used as a close support cannon or as an anti-tank gun.

31
The Swedish Bofors 40 mm light Anti-aircraft gun, one of the immortals.
Developed in 1929 it has since been adopted throughout the world,
built in other countries under licence, and in improved form is still
among the leading weapons of its type.

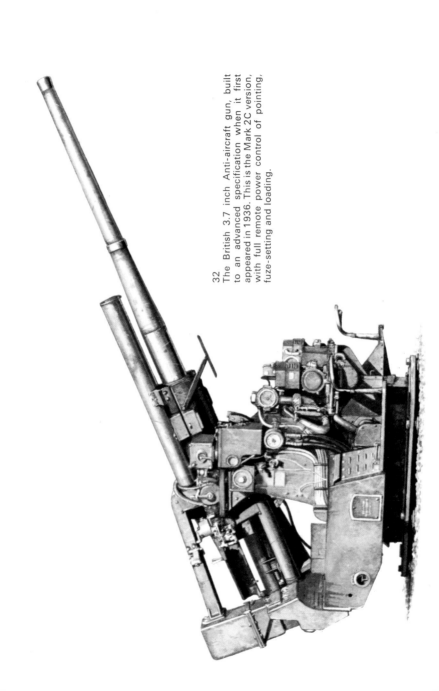

32
The British 3.7 inch Anti-aircraft gun, built to an advanced specification when it first appeared in 1936. This is the Mark 2C version, with full remote power control of pointing, fuze-setting and loading.

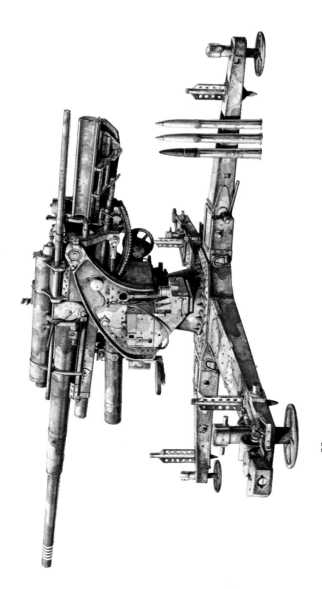

33
The famous German 'Eighty-Eight', the 8.8 cm Flak 36 Anti-aircraft gun, which proved to be as formidable as a field gun and anti-tank gun as it was in its primary role. In front of the outrigger leg are two HE rounds and an armour-piercing shell round.

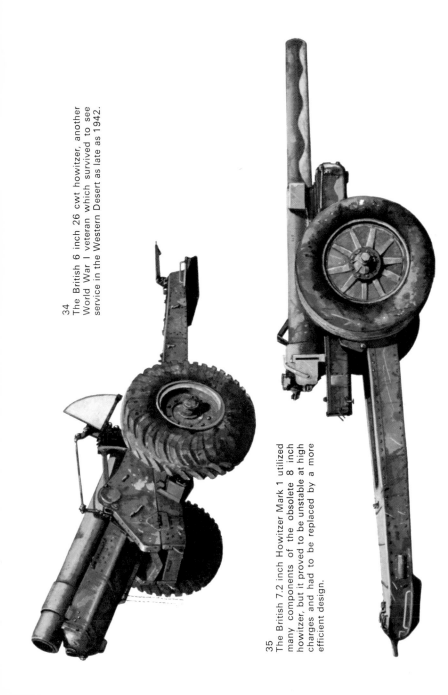

34
The British 6 inch 26 cwt howitzer, another World War I veteran which survived to see service in the Western Desert as late as 1942.

35
The British 7.2 inch Howitzer Mark 1 utilized many components of the obsolete 8 inch howitzer, but it proved to be unstable at high charges and had to be replaced by a more efficient design.

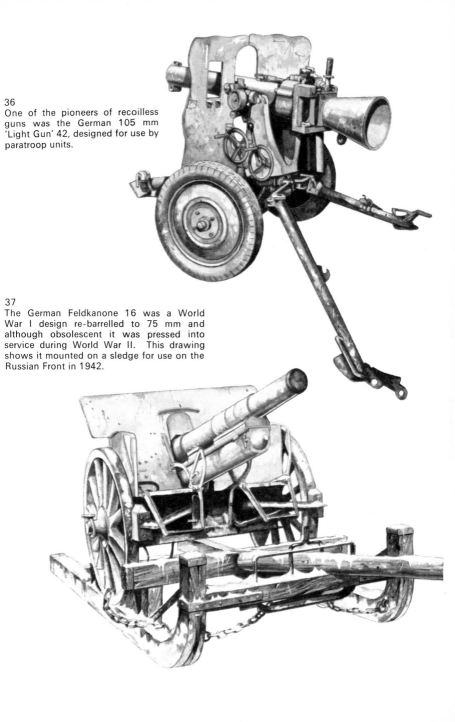

36
One of the pioneers of recoilless guns was the German 105 mm 'Light Gun' 42, designed for use by paratroop units.

37
The German Feldkanone 16 was a World War I design re-barrelled to 75 mm and although obsolescent it was pressed into service during World War II. This drawing shows it mounted on a sledge for use on the Russian Front in 1942.

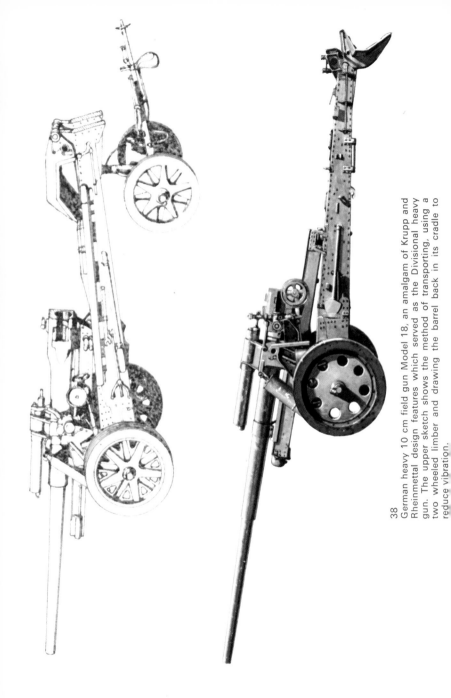

38

German heavy 10 cm field gun Model 18, an amalgam of Krupp and Rheinmettal design features which served as the Divisional heavy gun. The upper sketch shows the method of transporting, using a two wheeled limber and drawing the barrel back in its cradle to reduce vibration.

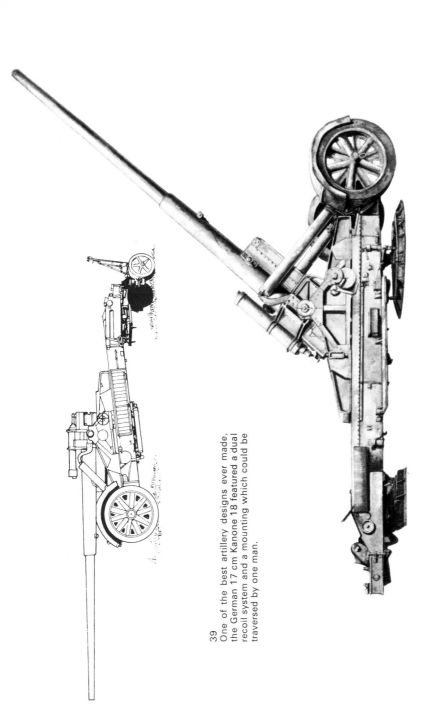

39
One of the best artillery designs ever made, the German 17 cm Kanone 18 featured a dual recoil system and a mounting which could be traversed by one man.

40
The US 155 mm Howitzer M1 was developed to replace the M 1917 in 1940. It was later fitted to self-propelled mountings and is still in use throughout the world.

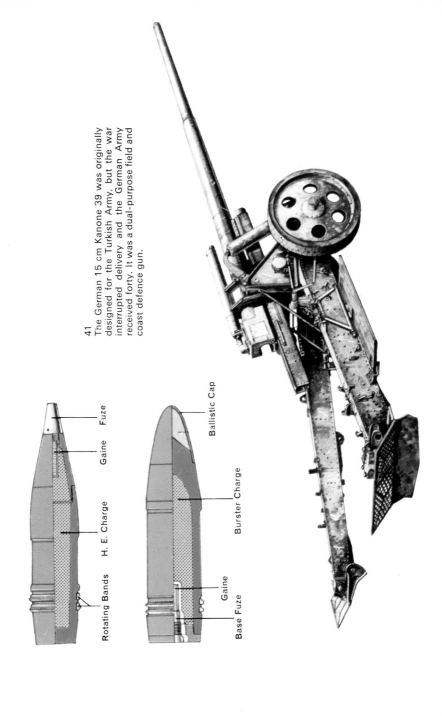

41
The German 15 cm Kanone 39 was originally designed for the Turkish Army, but the war interrupted delivery and the German Army received forty. It was a dual-purpose field and coast defence gun.

Fuze

Gaine

H. E. Charge

Rotating Bands

Ballistic Cap

Burster Charge

Gaine

Base Fuze

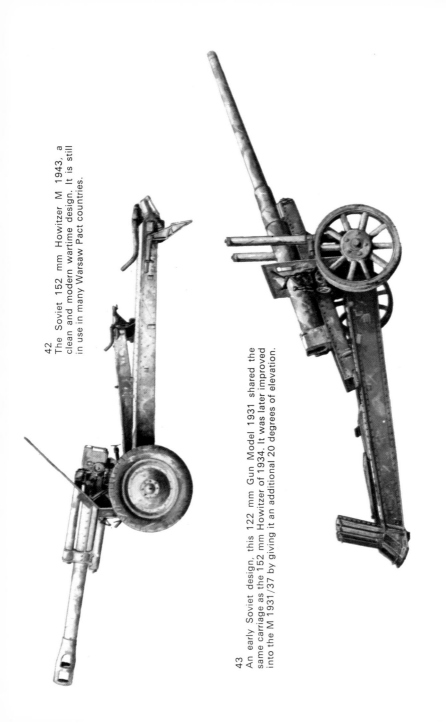

42
The Soviet 152 mm Howitzer M 1943, a clean and modern wartime design. It is still in use in many Warsaw Pact countries.

43
An early Soviet design, this 122 mm Gun Model 1931 shared the same carriage as the 152 mm Howitzer of 1934. It was later improved into the M 1931/37 by giving it an additional 20 degrees of elevation.

44
The German 15 cm Heavy Infantry Gun 33, the largest infantry gun ever issued, but one with a devastating short-range punch for instant support of the front line soldiers.

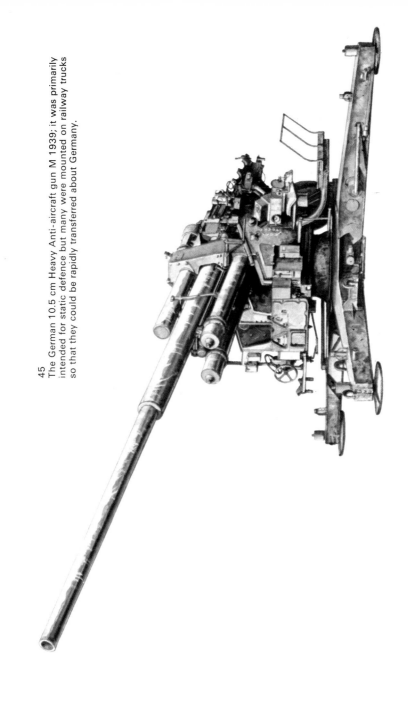

45
The German 10.5 cm Heavy Anti-aircraft gun M 1939; it was primarily intended for static defence but many were mounted on railway trucks so that they could be rapidly transferred about Germany.

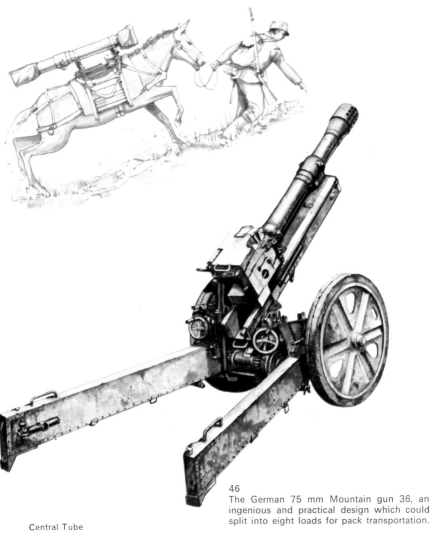

46
The German 75 mm Mountain gun 36, an ingenious and practical design which could split into eight loads for pack transportation.

Central Tube

Gaine   Burster Charge   Cup   Air Space

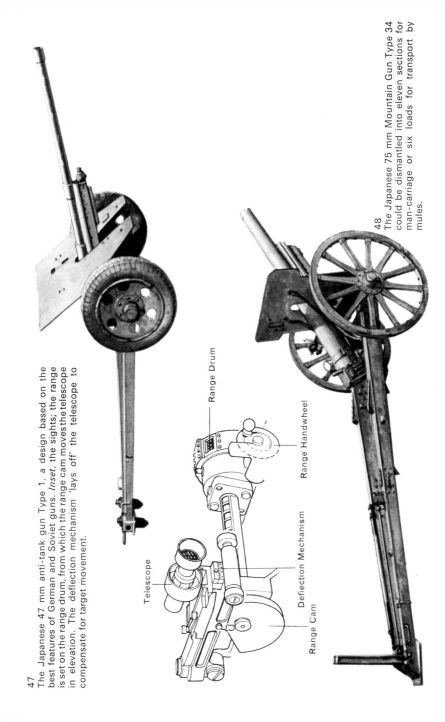

47
The Japanese 47 mm anti-tank gun Type 1, a design based on the best features of German and Soviet guns. *Inset*, the sights; the range is set on the range drum, from which the range cam moves the telescope in elevation. The deflection mechanism 'lays off' the telescope to compensate for target movement.

Range Drum

Telescope

Range Handwheel

Deflection Mechanism

Range Cam

48
The Japanese 75 mm Mountain Gun Type 34 could be dismantled into eleven sections for man-carriage or six loads for transport by mules.

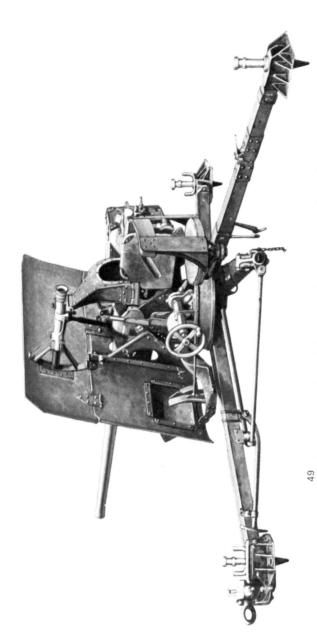

49
The British 2 pounder anti-tank gun, shown here in action with wheels removed, was a luxurious design giving full 360 degrees traverse.

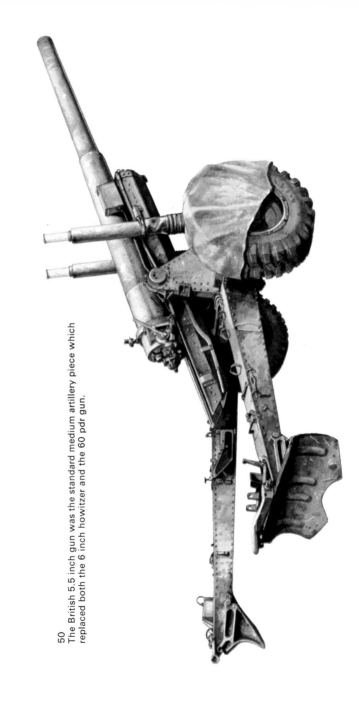

50
The British 5.5 inch gun was the standard medium artillery piece which replaced both the 6 inch howitzer and the 60 pdr gun.

51
The British 17 pounder anti-tank gun, which proved to be the most formidable weapon of its class on the Allied side during the war, particularly when provided with discarding sabot ammunition.

52
The US 75 mm Pack Howitzer M8 began life as a mule pack weapon but became pre-eminent as an airborne artillery piece in both British and American formations.

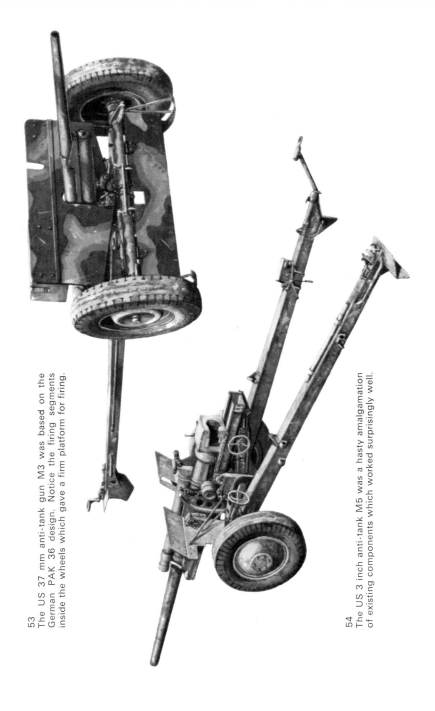

53
The US 37 mm anti-tank gun M3 was based on the German PAK 36 design. Notice the firing segments inside the wheels which gave a firm platform for firing.

54
The US 3 inch anti-tank M5 was a hasty amalgamation of existing components which worked surprisingly well.

55
The British 6 pounder anti-tank gun was designed in 1938 but was not produced until 1942, by which time it was desperately needed. The same gun was adopted by the US Army as their '57 mm Gun M1'.

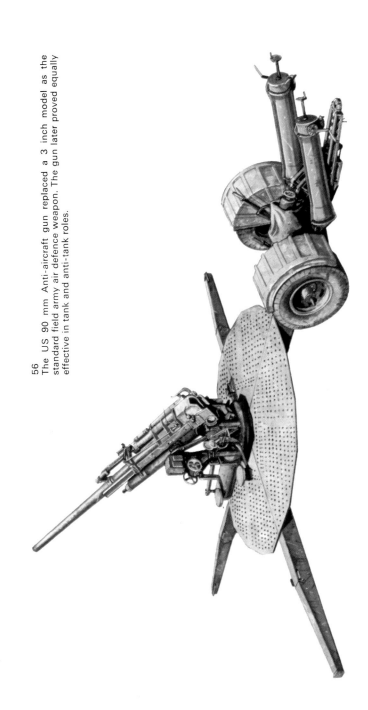

56
The US 90 mm Anti-aircraft gun replaced a 3 inch model as the standard field army air defence weapon. The gun later proved equally effective in tank and anti-tank roles.

57
The German SPzB41 2.8 cm anti-tank gun was the first service weapon ever to employ a tapering bore, the exit calibre being 21 mm.

58
The German 5 cm PAK 38, which appeared too late for the Polish and French campaigns.

59

A hastily-arranged marriage between a French gun and a German carriage brought about this 7.5 cm PAK 97/38, an attempt to provide sufficient anti-tank guns for the Russian front. *Inset* is a typical hollow-charge shell in part section.

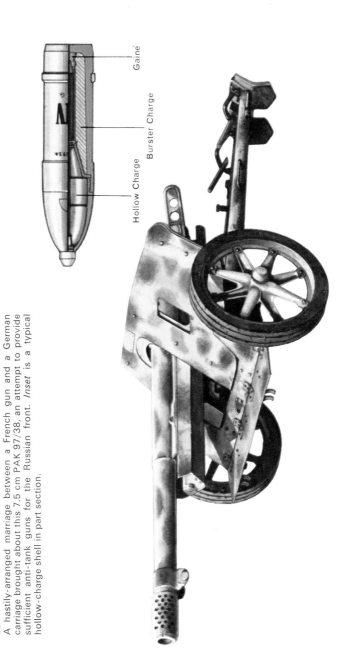

Hollow Charge

Burster Charge

Gainé

60
The Soviet 76.2 mm Divisional Gun M 1936 was modified by the Germans to become a useful addition to their anti-tank strength.

61
After using their 88 mm Anti-aircraft gun against tanks with great success, the Germans developed this 88 mm PAK 43 as a specialist anti-tank gun; it did great execution, particularly in Russia.

62
The German 24 cm Kanone 3 long range gun, an expensive and complicated weapon of which only six entered service.

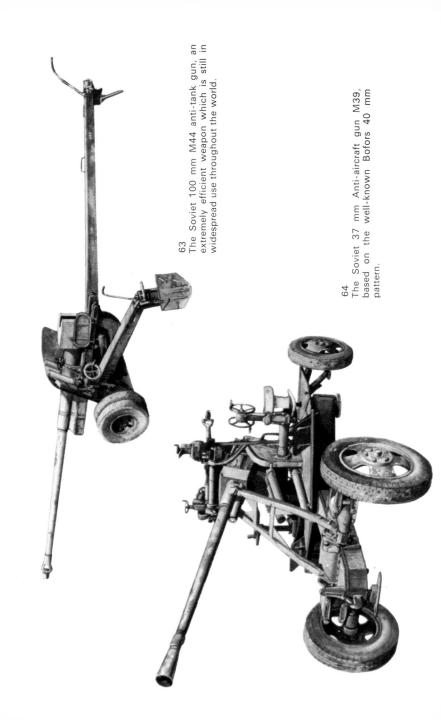

63
The Soviet 100 mm M44 anti-tank gun, an extremely efficient weapon which is still in widespread use throughout the world.

64
The Soviet 37 mm Anti-aircraft gun M39, based on the well-known Bofors 40 mm pattern.

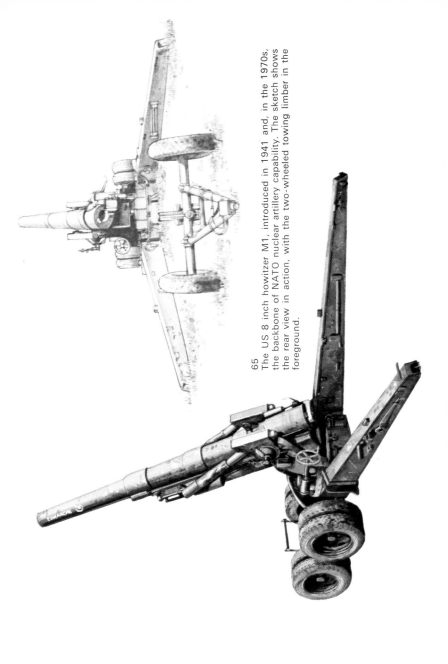

65
The US 8 inch howitzer M1, introduced in 1941 and, in the 1970s, the backbone of NATO nuclear artillery capability. The sketch shows the rear view in action, with the two-wheeled towing limber in the foreground.

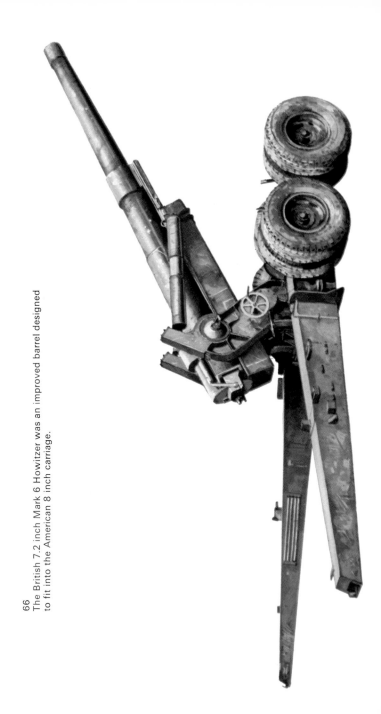

66
The British 7.2 inch Mark 6 Howitzer was an improved barrel designed
to fit into the American 8 inch carriage.

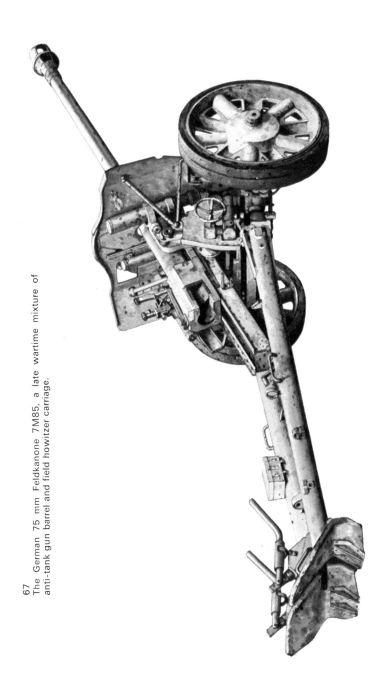

67
The German 75 mm Feldkanone 7M85, a late wartime mixture of anti-tank gun barrel and field howitzer carriage.

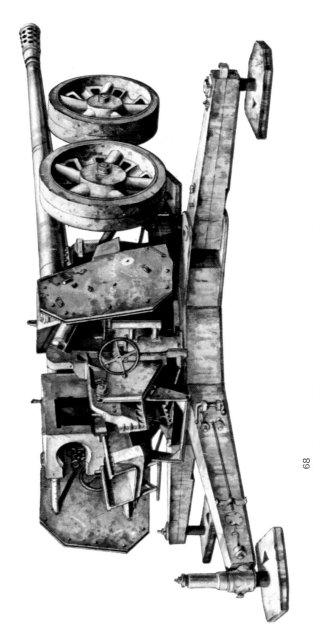

68
The German PAK 44 12.8 cm anti-tank gun, Rheinmettal-Borsig pattern, which arrived on the battlefield too late to be effective.

69
The US M3 105 mm howitzer was developed as an air-portable version of their standard field-piece. It was also tried as an infantry cannon, but this was not successful and it was then used only by airborne units.

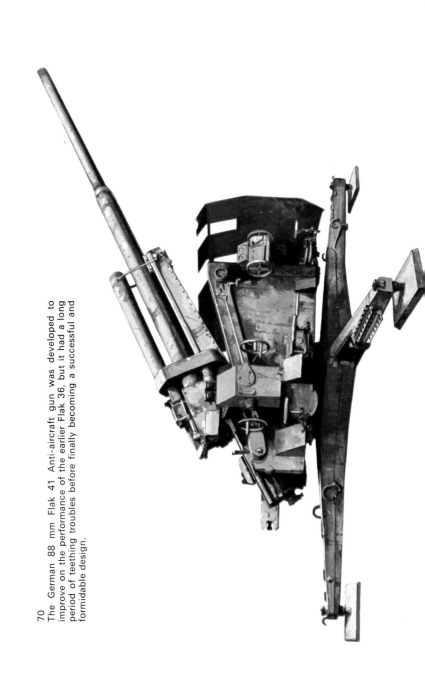

70
The German 88 mm Flak 41 Anti-aircraft gun was developed to improve on the performance of the earlier Flak 36, but it had a long period of teething troubles before finally becoming a successful and formidable design.

71
The German 88 mm PAK 43/41 was the PAK 43 barrel mounted on a
field howitzer carriage in order to get sufficient guns into action at
short notice. It was a cumbersome device but packed a terrible punch.

Fuze

Gaine

Burster Charge

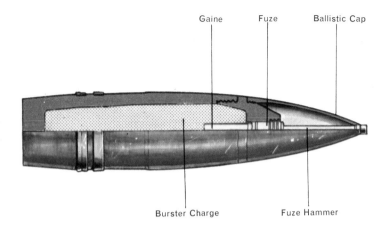

Gaine   Fuze   Ballistic Cap

Burster Charge   Fuze Hammer

72
The German 17 cm Kanone (Eisenbahn) railway gun ready to travel,
with a high explosive shell and, *inset* the method of emplacing it and
stabilizing by outriggers when firing across the track.

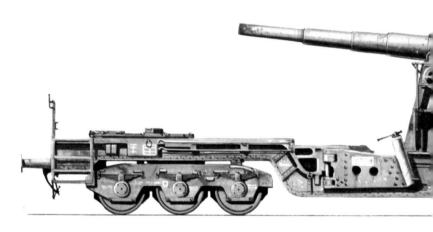

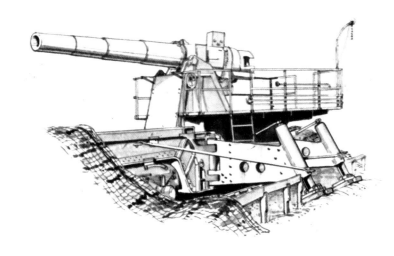

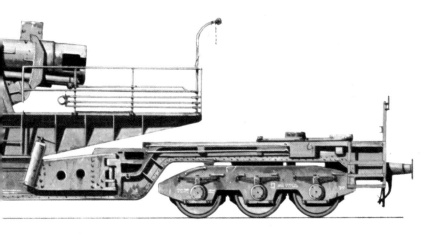

73
Gustav; the German 80 cm railway gun which fired a 7 ton shell to 23 miles range to devastate Sevastopol. *Inset*, the shell and cartridge with a crew member giving scale.

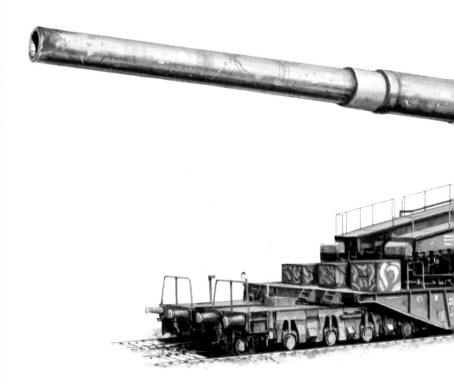

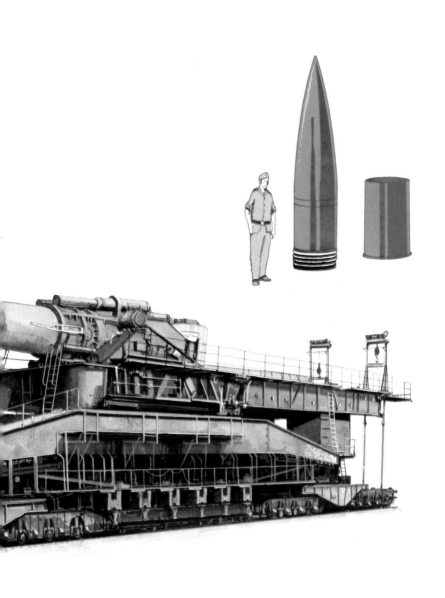

74
The British Smith Gun, a smooth bore 3 inch gun produced for the
Home Guard in 1940. To fire, it was tipped over, on to the concave
wheel which then became a traversing platform while the other wheel
acted as a shield.

75
The Australian-developed 'Short' 25 pounder field gun, produced
in order to get firepower through the jungles of New Guinea. The
'caster wheel' on the trail aided manoeuvring in confined spaces.

76
The Italian 105/56 Pack Howitzer, widely adopted by NATO armies in the 1950s. It can be used either as a field piece or as an anti-tank weapon.

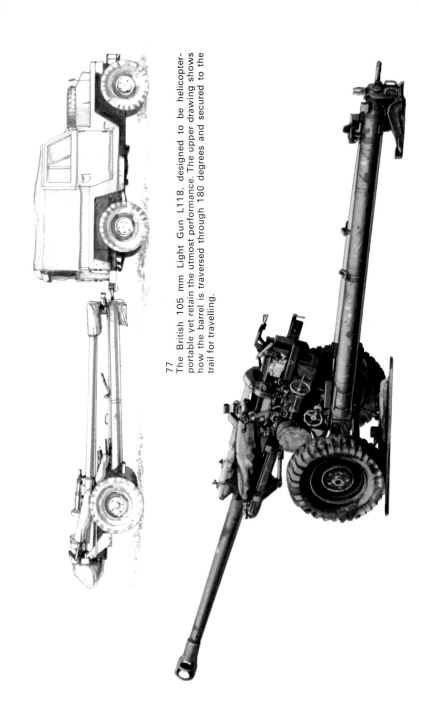

77
The British 105 mm Light Gun L118, designed to be helicopter-portable yet retain the utmost performance. The upper drawing shows how the barrel is traversed through 180 degrees and secured to the trail for travelling.

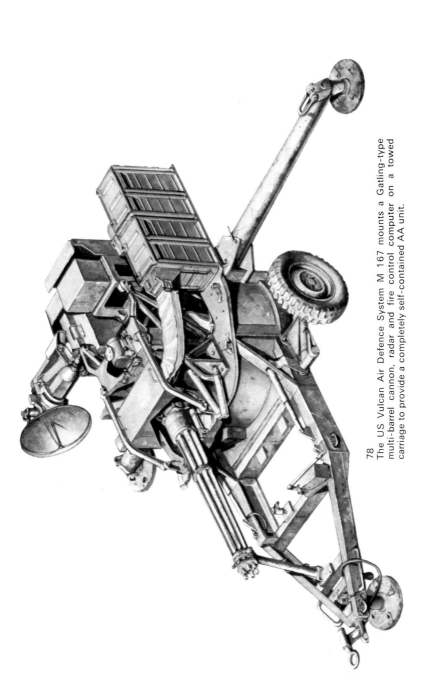

78
The US Vulcan Air Defence System M 167 mounts a Gatling-type
multi-barrel cannon, radar and fire control computer on a towed
carriage to provide a completely self-contained AA unit.

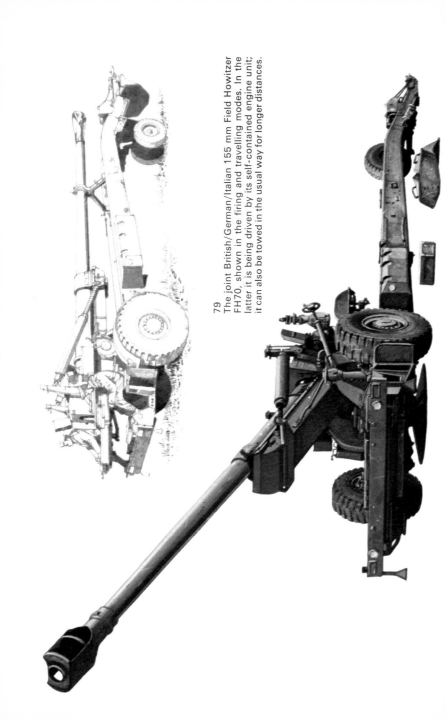

79
The joint British/German/Italian 155 mm Field Howitzer FH70, shown in the firing and travelling modes. In the latter it is being driven by its self-contained engine unit; it can also be towed in the usual way for longer distances.

went to the army in the desert where, in addition to their standard high explosive shells, they were provided with armour-piercing shot. Bigger, heavier and with better destructive range, these projectiles could reach out and destroy German armour at ranges the 2 pounder could not contemplate. Shot, though, was in short supply, and many of the early engagements saw the British guns using high explosive shells against tanks; in theory, these should not have had much effect, but in practice they were found to be highly effective, frequently dislodging the turret from some of the lighter German tanks.

The Germans now produced two surprises, forerunners of many more. In the Halfaya Pass battle in June 1941 the Germans brought their 88 mm anti-aircraft guns forward, dug them into the ground so as to be almost invisible, and used them with devastating effect as anti-tank guns, cutting the British armour to shreds. Shortly afterwards they brought into use a totally new concept in artillery, a gun with a tapered barrel. This was the 2.8 cm 'Schweres Panzerbuchse 41'; the term means 'heavy anti-tank rifle' but it was a small artillery piece, mounted upon wheels. The calibre at the breech was 28 mm, and the barrel then tapered until the calibre at the muzzle was 20 mm. As might be expected, the design of a suitable projectile to conform to this reduction in calibre was not simple; it involved using a body suited to the smaller calibre and then fitting it with 'skirts' of the larger calibre, the skirts being of soft metal so that they were deformed and squeezed down during passage through the bore. The object of all this was to give the projectile additional velocity; in simple terms, if the pressure on the base of the projectile, developed by the propellant gas, remains constant, then if the area of the projectile base is diminished the unit pressure per square centimetre of area increases and the projectile must be pushed faster. It was the perfection of an idea which had been patented in the opening years of the century and which had been gradually developed in the late

1920s and early 1930s by a German ordnance engineer called Gerlich.

There was one possible drawback to this idea, and that was the probability of a steel projectile breaking up on impact with the tank instead of penetrating the armour. Experiments showed that when a steel projectile arrived at an armoured target at high velocity – about 840 metres a second, or 2,750 feet a second was the critical velocity – it merely shattered on contact. The only answer to this was to make the projectile of some harder substance, and tungsten carbide was chosen. But tungsten carbide is considerably heavier than steel, so that a normal shot made of tungsten could not be fired at high velocity since it would not accelerate so fast in the gun. In the case of the Gerlich weapon, however, tungsten could be used for the small-calibre basic projectile, while the skirts could be very light, so that the whole shot still weighed very little and could be fired at extremely high velocity – the 28 mm gun developed 1,400 m/sec (4,590 ft/sec) and could pierce 66 mm (2.6 inches) of armour at 500 metres range, a formidable performance for such a tiny weapon.

The advantages of this system were obvious and the Germans went on to develop a 42 mm/29 mm gun followed by a 75 mm/55 mm gun, both of which were highly effective. At the same time they began experimenting with ways of adapting the tungsten projectile to a normal, parallel-bore, gun. Their solution was to take the Gerlich shot and turn it into a non-deforming design; the basic section was a small-calibre steel sheath containing a tungsten core, supported in the barrel by two enlarged sections. The side view of the resulting shot led to it being nicknamed 'Arrowhead' shot and it became standard issue for the 50 mm tank and anti-tank guns. At short ranges it was highly effective, but at long ranges it was less so, since the ratio of weight to cross-sectional area was low and thus the shot lacked 'carrying power'.

The British had known of the theories of Gerlich for many

years; indeed, he had done some development work in Britain on a high-velocity rifle for snipers in the early 1930s, but this came to nothing and it was generally believed that there was little practical worth in his ideas. A Czech engineer named Janacek, who had fled to Britain, had tried to promote the same system with little success until one of the German guns was captured in the desert and returned to Britain for examination. Janacek then offered to develop a simple screw-on, taper-bore attachment for the 2 pounder which, in conjunction with a special deforming shot, would considerably improve its performance. He eventually produced this device, known as the 'Littlejohn Adapter', but by the time it was perfected the 2 pounder was no longer in use as a field anti-tank gun and the Adapter was used only on armoured cars and light tanks.

For the 6 pounder a tungsten-cored 'Composite Rigid' shot was developed, similar to the German 'Arrowhead' shot but with a smooth outline. By the time that had been perfected, though, a better idea was in the offing and few of these were ever issued for service.

Another new idea which appeared in service at about this time was the hollow charge shell, also called the Shaped Charge or 'HEAT' (High Explosive, Anti-Tank) shell. In the latter part of the nineteenth century it had been observed that if an explosive charge were hollowed out and then detonated with the hollowed portion in contact with a steel plate, the dimensions of the hollow were reproduced in the plate. Various experimenters had tried to turn this into a viable weapon without much success. In 1914 a German experimenter found that by lining the hollow with a thin metal plate he could improve the performance to the point of piercing the target. Interest in the idea dwindled after 1919, but in 1938 two Swiss experimenters perfected a rifle grenade using this principle and attempted to sell it to various nations. This led to a revival of interest in the idea, and by 1940 both Britain and Germany had managed to develop working

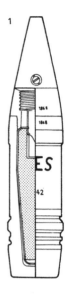

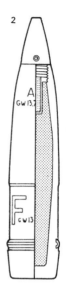

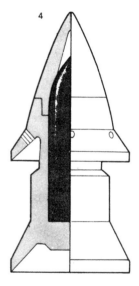

Typical German projectiles: 1) High explosive shell for a 75 mm field gun; 2) High explosive shell for a 75 mm field howitzer; note that due to the lower stresses, more explosive can be carried; 3) A hollow charge anti-tank shell for use with 105 mm field and recoilless guns; the nose fuze activates a primer at the rear end, which then initiates detonation of the hollow charge; 4) An 'Arrow-head' tungsten-cored shot used with the 28 mm taper-bore gun; the holes in the forward skirt are to prevent air being trapped as the shot is squeezed in the barrel.

munitions; Britain a rifle grenade, and Germany an artillery shell.

The hollow charge shell relied for its action upon the detonating force of the explosive carried within it. As the shell struck, so a fuze would detonate the explosive at the end remote from the shaped cavity at the front. The detonation wave, passing forward, would melt the metal lining of the cavity and force it into a high-speed jet of molten metal and explosive gas which was then directed against the armour plate of the target. This jet, moving at some 25,000 feet a second (7,600 m/sec) would force its way through the metal of the target and would then eject a jet of flame and molten metal into the interior of the tank, a jet capable of igniting fuel or ammunition or of killing a man. The operation of the shell was completely independent of range or velocity; provided the shell was brought into contact with the target, its effect was certain. Consequently, it was the ideal anti-tank projectile for low-velocity weapons such as light field guns and tank guns which were incapable of firing hard shot at the high velocities required to effect penetration by simple shock action.

Experience was to show, however, that there was a technical drawback to the use of hollow charge shells. In Britain, work began on developing a suitable design for the 25 pounder gun; at that time the fundamental principles behind the hollow charge were not particularly well understood, and much basic research was done, in the course of which it was found that when a hollow charge was spun at high speed, as in an artillery shell, the jet tended to thicken and dissipate its force due to the effect of centrifugal forces acting on the dense metallic portion of the jet. This meant that the jet made a wider hole but one of less depth, and frequently failed to penetrate armour which a static jet could pierce with ease. As a result, the British (and later the Americans) tended to concentrate their hollow charge development into un-spun projectiles, such as those used with infantry anti-tank devices and rocket launchers; apart from two American shells (for their 75 mm and 105 mm field weapons) and one British shell (for the 3.7 inch mountain howitzer) Allied hollow charge development passed from the artillery sphere.

*   *   *

In the late summer of 1940 the German Army had begun construction of several heavy artillery batteries on the coast of France with the intention of bombarding shipping in the English Channel and also of shelling south-eastern England. Most of these weapons were quite conventional and the brunt of the bombardment was taken by the Dover–Folkestone area of Kent which soon became known as 'Shell-Fire Corner'. But late in 1940 a shell landed at Rainham, near Chatham, in Kent, some 88 km (55 miles) from the nearest point on the French coast. This was well beyond the scope of the usual sort of gun and, after examination of the fragments, British technical experts postulated a German gun of immense power specially designed for extreme long-range bombardment. Although the war was to end before they had all their estimates proved correct, they were remarkably accurate in their calculations. The weapon they had thus discovered was the German 21 cm (8.26 inch) Kanone 12 Railway Gun.

During 1918 the German Navy had developed and manned the famous 'Kaiser Wilhelm Geschütz', better known as the 'Paris Gun', which had shelled Paris from a range of 76 miles. This rather upset the German Army, who considered that sailors were better employed floating about in ships than manning railway guns, and in the early 1920s they set about planning a long-range weapon which would relegate the Paris Gun to second place in history. Ballistic theory showed that it was necessary to develop a very high muzzle velocity in order to throw the shell into the stratosphere where, with less air resistance, it would travel much farther than in the normal atmosphere. To do this, however, led to mechanical problems, particularly in respect of spinning the shell; the conventional driving band, pressed into the shell body, which deformed into the rifling and gave the shell the necessary spin, would never stand up to the pressures and velocities required in this application. The solution arrived at was to rifle the gun not with the usual shallow grooves but with a small number of very deep grooves, and then manufacture the shell with suitably curved ribs which would fit into the grooves and thus distribute the rotational force more evenly through the walls of the shell. A soft metal driving band would be provided at the rear in order to seal the propellant gases, but this would play no part in the spinning action. Tests on a number of experimental 105 mm barrels showed that an eight-grooved barrel gave the necessary performance, and in 1935 work began on the full-calibre gun.

The other requirement for high velocity is a long barrel which allows the propellant gases to develop their full thrust, and the barrel for this weapon had to be 33.3 m (109 ft 3 ins) long. Such an enormous length was liable to bend under its own weight, and thus a system of trusses had to be designed to keep the tube perfectly straight. It was thought impossible to balance this enormous length of barrel by springs or any other agency, and so the trunnions, about which the gun elevated, were set as far forward as possible to reduce the muzzle preponderance. This, in turn, meant that when the gun was elevated the breech would touch the ground and leave little or no room for recoil. To solve this, the railway mounting was a complicated structure; it was basically a large box carried on two double bogies, and within the box was a hydraulic recoil system carrying the gun cradle. Within the cradle was a second recoil system connected to the gun barrel. The basic box was then coupled to hydraulic jacks so that before firing the whole mounting was lifted one metre into the air above the bogies so as to give additional clearance for the breech to recoil. When the gun fired, the gun itself recoiled within the cradle, while the cradle also recoiled within the mounting body. The whole equipment weighed 297 tons, stood 41.3 m (139.5 ft) long and fired a 107.5 kg (237 lb) shell at a velocity of 1500 m/sec (4920 ft/sec) to a range of 115 km (71.5 miles). One complete gun, known as the K12(V) was built and issued in 1938. Practical experience showed that there were some features which the Army did not like, notably the business of having to jack it up and down for every shot, and a second model was then built, the K12(N) in which the trunnions were set farther back and a hydro-pneumatic cylinder arrangement balanced the muzzle weight. Other minor changes were made and this differed from the earlier version by weighing 318,000 kg (313 tons) and being 44.95 m (147.6 ft) long, though its performance was the same.

These two guns cost 3,000,000 Reichsmarks – about £267,000 at the 1939 rate of exchange. They were issued to Eisenbahn Artillerie Abteilung 701 and in 1940 the unit went to France where one gun was emplaced and opened fire; when the barrel became worn, the gun was withdrawn for repair and the second weapon brought into action. Some time in 1941 they were withdrawn and their subsequent movements are a mystery; neither of them survived the war. Even Krupp's engineers later admitted that as practical weapons of war they were nonsense, but as research tools they were claimed to have been worth every penny spent upon them.

While the K12(V) was opening fire on England, two other extremes of artillery giantism were going forward in the German gunshops, both of which had been begun in 1937. The first of these to be completed was a massive self-propelled equipment known as the 60 cm 'Karl', which had been demanded by the Army in order to bring heavy fire-power to bear on fortifications out of reach of railway artillery. It consisted of a tracked chassis supporting a simple box hull, upon which was a dual recoil mounting carrying the 60 cm (23.6 inch) howitzer. This fired a 1,576 kg (3,476 lb) high explosive shell to 6,675 m (7,300 yards) or a 2,195 kg (4,840 lb) concrete-piercing shell to 4,480 m (4,900 yards). As might be imagined, these shells had a devastating effect on impact, the concrete-piercing shell being able to pass through 2.5 m (8 feet) of reinforced concrete. Six equipments were built in 1940–41 but the Army were disappointed in the range and Rheinmetall-Borsig, the makers, developed six 54 cm (21.25 inch) barrels which could be interchanged with the 60 cm barrels; these fired a 1,247 kg (2,750 lb) shell to a range of 12,500 m (13,670 yards) and with that the Army was content. The six equipments were sent to Russia in July 1941 and were used to bombard the fortress of Brest-Litovsk, then moved to Lvov and later took part in the siege of Sevastopol in 1942.

The other great gun was a private venture by the Krupp company; in 1936 Hitler had enquired of Krupp how big a gun would be needed to defeat the fortifications of the Maginot Line and in 1937 Gustav Krupp had given instructions for designs of an 80 cm (31.5 inch) railway gun to be drawn up. When they were completed he laid them in front of the Army, who approved, and then began building it. It was promised for the spring of 1940 but the construction of such a massive weapon turned out to be more difficult than even Krupp's had thought, and it was not until late in 1940 that the barrel was completed and proof-fired. The whole weapon was not finished before March 1942, when it was tested in Hitler's presence. It was christened 'Gustav' in honour of the ruling member of the Krupp house, and was presented to Hitler as Krupp's contribution to the war effort. The German gunners, less reverently, called it 'Dora'.

Although there have been weapons of greater calibre, no gun has ever surpassed Gustav for sheer size. When assembled it straddled two railway tracks, stood 43 m (141 ft) long, 7 m (23 ft) wide and 11.6 m (38 ft) high, and weighed 1,350,000 kg (1,329 tons). It seems hardly necessary to point out that it had to be moved piecemeal, using special trains, and assembled on site by cranes, a process which took up to three weeks. Two types of shell were provided, a high explosive shell of 4,800 kg (4.73 tons) which had a velocity of 820 m/sec (2,690 ft/sec) and a range of 47 km (29.2 miles), and a concrete-piercing shell of 7,100 kg (6.9 tons) with a velocity of 710 m/sec (2,330 ft/sec) and a range of 38 km (23.6 miles).

After testing, Gustav was sent to join the siege of Sevastopol, where it fired a number of shells, variously reported as being between 36 and 55; it was then sent to Leningrad, but the siege there ended before it could be got into action. It was later reputed to have fired a few rounds into Warsaw during the 1944 rising, but apart from that it was never used, and its contribution to the war effort must be considered minimal.

*   *   *

The Western Allies chose not to involve themselves in such grandiose projects as Karl and Gustav; their requirements were more pedestrian, since due to their late start in rearming their first priority was to equip their expanding armies with the standard field and medium weapons which would give the necessary support to their armies in the field. In Britain the problem was made even worse by the need, in prewar days, to produce sufficient anti-aircraft guns to defend the country against the threat of bombers from the continent, and this had swallowed up much of the available finance and manufacturing capacity before 1939. The result, though, was worthwhile, since the military specifications drawn up as far back as 1928 had resulted, in 1936, in the 3.7 inch (94 mm) anti-aircraft gun, a very advanced design for its day. It carried no optical sights, being intended to have data transmitted to it from fire control instruments and displayed on dials; all the gunlayer had to do was operate his controls and move the gun until pointers on the dials actuated by the gun's movement coincided with pointers set by the fire control instruments. It fired a 28 lb (12.7 kg) shell at 2,600 ft/sec (792 m/sec) to a height of 41,000 feet (12,500 m). This statement should be qualified by a brief explanation of how the performance of anti-aircraft guns was rated. The 41,000 feet quoted above was the maximum height to which the gun could have projected a shell against the pull of gravity; but this is a spurious figure, since the real shell had a time fuze which would burst the shell after a maximum time of flight of 43 seconds. Moreover, even this figure was of little value, since it assumed the gun was at its maximum elevation of 80 degrees, and a moment's thought will show that only one shot against a moving aircraft could be fired at that angle. Once the aircraft had moved, the gun's angle would have to change and thus the maximum height of the bursting shell would change. In view of all these conflicting 'maximum heights', an 'effective ceiling' was calculated, which was that height at which it would be able to engage a target for a worthwhile length of time, say twenty or thirty seconds. In the case of the 3.7 inch gun, this effective ceiling was 32,000 feet (9,750 m).

The 3.7 inch gun was originally designed as a mobile equipment, travelling on four wheels which were removed when it went into action, but this carriage was a complicated design and to speed things up a simpler static mounting was devised, suitable for anchoring in concrete for the defence of cities, factories and harbours. To deter the low-level raider and to provide cover for the field armies, quantities of the 40 mm Bofors gun were purchased before the war, and a licence to manufacture was obtained so that the gun could be produced in Britain and Canada.

With the anti-aircraft defences barely begun (though they were not up to full strength until the middle of the war) there was time to look at the other needs of the field armies. Primary among these was the provision of a modern gun to replace the old 6 inch medium gun and 6 inch medium howitzers, both of which were of World War I design and feeling their age. In January 1939 a design of 5 inch gun had been worked out, but it was found that the best ballistic promise was in a slightly larger calibre, and it became the 5.5 inch (140 mm) gun instead. This was a modern split-trail carriage with hydraulic balancing gear to take the weight of the muzzle, and with a complicated breech mechanism. Unfortunately the design was a little too clever, and the hydraulic balancing gear had to be replaced by a spring pattern in the interests of simplicity and reliability, while the complex breech and firing mechanism also had to be abandoned in favour of a more simple design. All this took time, and it was not until May 1942 that the 5.5 inch gun finally reached the hands of the troops in North Africa. It fired a 100 lb (45.3 kg) shell to a range of 16,200 yards (14,810 m) and was very successful and well-liked. But later, during the Italian campaign, it developed a sudden and lethal tendency to detonate its shell prematurely, in the barrel as soon as the firing lanyard was pulled. This gave it a bad reputation which took some time to live down, but it was eventually traced to an unfortunate combination of minor defects and cured, after which the 5.5 gave no more trouble. In 1943 an 80 lb (36.3 kg) shell was introduced in order to extend the maximum range to 18,100 yards (16,550 m).

The 5.5 inch gun was accompanied by a 4.5 inch (114 mm) gun which, except for having a slightly longer barrel, was almost indistinguishable since it was carried on the same carriage. This had first been suggested as a cheap and simple conversion of the old 5 inch 60 pounder gun, simply a matter of re-lining the 60 pounder to 4.5 inches and giving it a new 55 lb (24.9 kg) shell so as to reach a range of 20,000 yards (18,290 m). The idea was tested in 1937 and shown to work; approval was given, after which it was discovered that there were only 76 60 pounders available to be converted, which hardly made it worth while. So in 1938 a new 4.5 inch barrel was requested, dimensioned so that it would be interchangeable with that of the 5.5 inch gun and thus be able to utilize the same carriage. This appeared in 1942 at much the same time as the 5.5 inch version, and was allocated so that each Medium Regiment RA had one battery of 5.5 inch and one of 4.5 inch. But the extra range of the 4.5 did not really compensate for the lighter shell, and once the 80 lb shell was made available to the 5.5 inch guns the 4.5 inch began to be phased out of service.

Development of heavier weapons during the pre-war years had been almost at a standstill, firstly because of the shortage of design staff and money, and secondly because of the oft-stated belief that in any future war the Royal Air Force would be able to take over the function of long range artillery. As war came closer, though, it was obvious that the RAF had neither the equipment nor the inclination to assist the field armies; their sights were set on strategic bombing and defending Britain, and who can blame them? So although some tentative specifications were drawn up for heavy artillery in 1938–39 nothing was done until 1940. At that time the only heavy field howitzer was the 8 inch, a design which had not been a particularly good one even when it was new, and it was decided to develop a new barrel which would fit the same carriage but give more range. After various experiments, 7.2 inches (184 mm) was settled on as the calibre, and the old 8 inch howitzers were re-lined with new barrels. The new weapon fired a 200 lb (90.7 kg) shell to 16,900 yards (15,450 m) but it was an alarming beast to see in action. The old-style box trail had two large balloon-tyred wheels, and since the force of recoil of the new barrel was rather more than the old 8 inch recoil system could absorb, the whole carriage would move back on firing. To limit this movement, massive wedges were placed behind the wheels, so that on recoil the wheels ran up the wedges, stopped and then ran down again, the gun bouncing as it returned to the ground. The placing of these wedges was the highest expression of the gun captain's art; too far, and the gun did not move far enough up the wedge and thus did not return to the proper place; too near, and the gun sailed up the wedge and over the top to crash to the ground. At the highest charge the howitzer was nearly uncontrollable, and in 1943 it was decided to start again on a completely new carriage design.

A NEED FOR NEW DESIGNS

In the United States the events of 1939–40 had at least loosened the purse-strings and money was available for the provision of weapons. The 105 mm howitzer, which had been gradually taking shape, was finally standardized in March 1940 and manufacture got under way, over 8,500 being built during the war. A 3 inch (76 mm) anti-tank gun was also put in hand, a hurried design using the barrel of an anti-aircraft gun allied to the modified carriage of the 105 mm howitzer; for all that it was hurried, it proved to be a highly efficient weapon, though its development was slowed by problems with designing an efficient piercing shell. But the most urgent need, like that of the British and for the same reasons, was in the medium and heavy artillery field. The pre-war army had been equipped with the French 155 mm gun and howitzer which the Americans had taken in 1917, and while both were still serviceable they were not up to modern standards of performance. New designs had been drawn up in the late 1920s, but it was not until 1939 that authority was given for them to be fully developed.

The M1917 155 mm howitzer was a short-barrelled weapon with a box trail and a particularly awkward system of traverse which relied upon moving the whole carriage across the axle by a worm and screw arrangement. The new design was a split trail carriage which allowed more elevation and traverse, and it was then completed by a new, longer, design of gun which gave a considerable gain in range. Firing

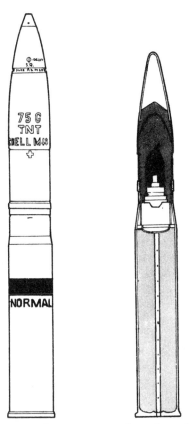

Left: typical markings on an American 75 mm gun round; Right: sectioned view of an armour-piercing shell with piercing and ballistic caps, for the 3 inch anti-tank gun.

a 95 lb (43 kg) shell at 1,850 ft/sec (564 m/sec) it had a maximum range of 16,355 yards (14,955 m), an improvement of almost 4,000 yards over the 1917 model.

The 155 mm gun went earlier into manufacture, having been standardized in 1938. This, too, used a split trail carriage but one of unusual design in which the weight, when towing, was borne by an eight-wheeled bogie. To emplace the gun the trails were opened and the bogie then lifted clear of the ground so that the carriage sat firmly on the ground and resisted any movement. The gun was 45 calibres long, instead of the 38 calibres of the M1917 model, and fired a 95 lb shell to 25,395 yards (23,220 m).

During World War I the British had a number of 8 inch howitzers built in the USA by contractors, and when their needs had been satisfied the contractors were told to keep going but make the weapons for the American Army. By 1939 these were well out of date and a new 8 inch howitzer was designed as a 'partner piece' to the 155 mm gun, so that it could utilize the same split-trail carriage. This was standardized in 1940 as the 8 inch howitzer M1, and fired a 200 lb (91 kg) shell to a range of 18,510 yards (16,925 m).

Numbers of both these weapons, the 155 mm gun M1 and the 8 inch howitzer M1, were shipped to Britain and it occurred to the British that in order to save time and effort, if these two American barrels could be interchanged in the same mounting, then it might be possible to adapt the same mounting to the 7.2 inch howitzer. Then came the thought that it would be rather a waste to place such an elegant mounting under the existing 7.2, which, after all, was a hasty conversion of an old 8 inch design. So in 1943 work began on designing a completely new 7.2 inch barrel, to be called the 'Mark 6', which had similar external dimensions at the critical points so that it could be interchanged with either of the American barrels. In December 1943 the new design was approved; it turned out to be an excellent weapon which outranged the earlier 7.2 inch designs by about two miles and, of course, was as steady as a rock on firing.

Having thus ensured the basic artillery support weapons, the Americans then turned to bigger things. Another memento of World War I was a 240 mm (9.45 inch) howitzer, an ungainly weapon which, like most of the howitzers of its era, was transported in pieces and laboriously assembled on site by means of hoists and gyns. It was not well-liked, and as early as 1925 tests had shown that the only hope of salvation was to scrap it and start again, but with 330 of them built there was little chance of that being permitted. Nevertheless, design studies were done; these were completed by about 1935 and then shelved until they could be used. This time came in 1939 and the new 240 mm Howitzer M1 was standardized in 1943. It was still, of course, far too big a weapon to be moved in one piece, but the design was very 'clean' and divided it into two sections, the barrel and cradle, and the mounting. Each of these was carried on a six-wheeled trailer, drawn by a special tracked tractor. Each complete howitzer was accompanied by a mobile crane with a bucket attachment; on arrival at the selected firing site the crane first dug the spade and recoil pits, then lifted the mounting and lowered it on to the pit, spreading the trail legs and attaching the spades. Then it lifted the barrel and cradle unit, lowered it into the mounting, where it was attached by four massive bolts, and the gun was ready for action. In this manner the whole equipment could be ready in about two hours. If the crane was not available, the pit had to be dug by hand and the weapon could then be emplaced using the winches on the towing tractors; this could take anything from eight hours upwards, depending upon the state of the ground.

During World War I the US Army had mounted a number of 8 inch coast guns on railway trucks for use on the Western Front, and in the 1920s they began to explore the possibility of producing a road-mobile mounting for the same gun. The idea was given a low priority and was abandoned, but in 1939

114

it was revived with the idea of producing another 'partner piece', this time an 8 inch gun barrel to fit into the same mounting as the 240 mm howitzer. Approval was given in June 1940 but it was not until 1944 that the gun was standardized, due to technical problems which arose during the development. The problem was principally one of excessive wear of the bore, which led to poor accuracy, and this was never completely solved. As a result, the 8 inch gun M1 was less frequently seen in service and it was phased out fairly quickly after the war. But these two 'partners' were formidable long range support weapons; the 240 mm howitzer fired a 360 lb (163 kg) shell to a range of 25,225 yards (23,065 m), while the 8 inch gun fired a 240 lb (109 kg) shell to 35,635 yards (32,585 m).

In the anti-aircraft field the Americans had long relied on a 3 inch derived from a World War I design, and a light 37 mm weapon designed by John M. Browning of machine-gun fame, but neither were fully satisfactory to cope with modern high-speed, high-altitude aircraft. The 37 mm was retained and used in a combination mounting with twin .50 machine-guns, but the Bofors 40 mm was adopted as the general light AA gun. To replace the 3 inch, a 90 mm gun of advanced design was developed in the late 1930s and approved for production in March 1940. This fired a time-fuzed 23 lb (10.4 kg) shell at 2,700 ft/sec (823 m/sec) to an effective ceiling of 33,800 feet (10,300 m) at a rate of 15 rounds a minute. In an attempt to speed up the rate of fire a spring-actuated rammer was developed and fitted, but it turned out to be a troublesome device; it increased the rate of fire to 25 rpm when it worked, but it was usually removed by the gunners as an alternative to constantly adjusting and repairing it. The 90 mm gun was mounted on a rather peculiar two-wheeled mounting which took some time to bring into action, and a fresh carriage design was requested, one which would allow the gun to be fired from its wheels in an emergency. This resulted in the M2 gun which appeared in

1943; it was ballistically the same but incorporated an excellent automatic rammer and fuze setter and the weapon was carried on a four-wheeled platform carriage with provision for controlling the gun electrically from the fire control director.

The 90 mm was highly mobile in either form, and served the field armies well, but a heavier and more powerful weapon was considered necessary for defence of the USA against possible attack. Such an attack would obviously be from very high altitude aircraft, and a 120 mm (4.7 inch) gun was developed in 1939–40. This used separate ammunition, the shell and cartridge being two distinct units, but an ingenious loader-fuze setter unit managed to produce a rate of fire of 12 rpm. The shell weighed 50 lbs (22.6 kg), had a velocity of 3,100 ft/sec (945 m/sec) and an effective ceiling of 47,400 feet (14,450 m).

The prospect of aircraft becoming faster and more difficult to hit had occurred to other nations as well, once the war had begun and the aircraft designers were vying with each other to produce bigger and better bombers. In January 1941 the British Army asked for a new anti-aircraft gun which would have a ceiling of 50,000 ft (15,250 m), a velocity which would put the shell up to that height in 30 seconds, and the ability to fire three shots and have a fourth loaded all within 20 seconds. Of the various solutions proposed, the long-term answer was to adopt a 5.25 inch (134 mm) gun which the Royal Navy already had in service; this, though, would take some considerable time to convert into a suitable form for land service – a complete new mounting would have to be developed – and as a short term answer an improved 3.7 inch gun was proposed. This was to be a completely new 65-calibre 3.7 inch barrel fitted into the jacket of the older 4.5 inch AA gun, itself an ex-Naval weapon. To produce the high velocity required, a new form of rifling was developed in which the bottom of the rifling grooves gradually came up to meet the top, thus converting the last few inches of the barrel into a smoothbore. To go with this, a special type of driving band was developed for the shell, so that as the rifling shallowed the copper of the driving band was squeezed into grooves in the shell body. Thus, when the shell left the gun muzzle the excrescenses of the driving band were smoothed away and the body of the projectile allowed a perfectly smooth airflow across its surface; the turbulence of the air flow caused by a conventional un-smoothed driving band robs a shell of a great deal of its velocity during flight, and this 'fairing-off' of the 3.7 inch shell was instrumental in maintaining the initial high velocity for a considerable part of the shell's flight. The weight of shell remained the same at 28 lbs (12.7 kg) but the velocity was increased from 2,600 ft/sec to 3,425 ft/sec (1,044 m/sec) and the maximum ceiling from 41,000 ft to 59,300 ft (18,075 m). Bearing in mind our previous observations on the various ceilings, the 'effective' ceiling of the new gun was 45,000 feet (13,700 m).

The Germans, with their usual prescience, had made early provision in order to keep ahead of aircraft improvements; at the end of 1933 they had demanded a 10.5 cm gun and in 1936 went even further and requested a 12.8 cm (5.03 inch) gun as well. Two prototypes of the 10.5 cm model were ordered, one from Krupp and one from Rheinmetall, each using different forms of power control. After tests of these pilot models, two experimental batteries were constructed, one for each type of gun, and thoroughly tested in 1936. Finally the Rheinmetall model, using hydraulic power control, was selected and put into production. A complex and ingenious loading mechanism was fitted in which the loader dropped a round into a loading tray, from where it was moved forward to the mechanical fuze setter and the fuze automatically set at the correct time to burst. The round then slid back on the tray, the tray rocked and tipped the round into a second tray, which then moved over and presented the tip of the shell to two spinning rollers in the breech. These then contracted, gripped the shell, and whisked it into the chamber; the breech closed, the tray moved back out of the path of recoil, and the gun fired. Meanwhile the loader had dropped a fresh round on to the loading tray and the cycle had already begun again. Using this mechanism a rate of fire of about 15 rounds a minute could be achieved, with rounds of ammunition which weighed 26.5 kg (58 lbs) each. As well as being widely emplaced throughout Germany for home defence, many of these 10.5 cm guns were specially mounted on railway trucks so that they could be rapidly moved around in order to increase the defences of any particular area at short notice.

The 12.8 cm was little more than an enlarged 10.5 cm gun, but the increase in size led to problems with transportation. It was necessary to remove the barrel from the gun and move it as a separate load; this system had been written into the original demand and approved in the trials of the pilot model, but practical use soon revealed that it was an impossible burden for a weapon which was supposed to be quick into action. Late in 1938 a one-load transport system, using a massive eight-wheeled trailer, was devised, but this led to a load which weighed 26,450 kg (26 tons) and was some 15 m (49 ft) long. Few of them were built, since it was decided that this was obviously a static weapon, not to be dragged around the country unnecessarily.

When the specification for the 12.8 cm gun was drawn up, one for an even larger weapon of 15 cm (5.9 inch) calibre was also approved; development of this continued for several years but never achieved a serviceable weapon for a variety of technical reasons. But in 1940, in the search for better and more effective anti-aircraft defences, the Germans began building 'flak towers' in their major cities, massive concrete citadels almost 40 m (130 feet) high, with the intention of mounting the 15 cm guns upon them so as to give them a clear field of fire in all directions. Even at that early date it seemed unlikely that the 15 cm guns would be ready for some considerable time, and a twin 12.8 cm gun equipment was developed and placed on the towers. The first was installed in

1942, and by the war's end 34 such twin equipments had been installed.

The 88 mm, it will be recalled, had been designed at the end of the 1920s, which meant that by the 1940s it was falling behind in the race, and a new 88 mm weapon was requested, one which could fire 25 rounds a minute at a muzzle velocity of not less than 1,000 m/sec (3,280 ft/sec). Design, by Rheinmetall-Borsig, had begun in 1939 but it moved slowly, bedevilled by technical problems and also by constant revision of the specification by the Luftwaffe. Eventually, late in 1942, it appeared as the '8.8 cm Flak 41' but its early days were not a success. The carriage design was excellent, a low-set affair with the gun mounted on a turntable instead of the usual high-set pedestal, but the gun barrel had been made in three sections, and the joint between two of these fell at the point where the cartridge case mouth rested. On firing, the case often expanded into this joint and jammed, failing to extract. The design of barrel was changed twice before the problem was finally solved, after which the Flak 41 had a successful career. Indeed, the Czechoslovakian Army acquired several after the war and continued to use them until the 1960s.

The German attack on Russia in 1941 was, at first, a runaway success, and vast amounts of booty fell into German hands. Among this were thousands of pieces of artillery, many of which were immediately put to use on the German side. Russian artillery in general resembled Japanese in that it was basic, rugged, and had a good performance allied to light weight. The basic divisional gun of the Red Army was a 76 mm (3 inch) weapon of which there were two principal models, the 1936 and the 1939; ballistically they were very similar, the 1936 having a maximum range of 13,330 m and the 1939 of 13,600 m, but the 1939 was a better mechanical job, had an improved recoil system and was rather lighter. So many of these were taken by the Germans that they found it feasible to make a few changes and adopt it as a service

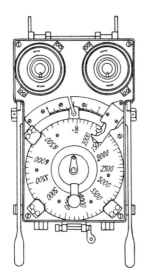

Bracket fuze setter, a typical machine used with French and German time fuzes at the beginning of the war; the shells were inserted nose first into the circular receptacles at the top, the dials set to the required range, and the levers pulled to set the fuzes.

A 'Telescope, Stereoscopic' used by artillery observers in most armies; this Japanese model shows it in use as a periscope; by opening the 'donkey's ears' the instrument could give an accentuated stereoscopic effect for long range observation.

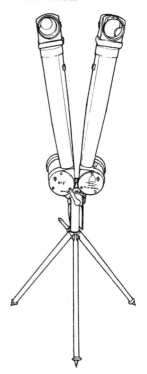

weapon. The chamber was enlarged to take a standard German cartridge case, the controls were altered to make the sights, elevation and traverse all under the control of one man, and a muzzle brake was added so that the performance could be stepped up slightly. With these changes it became the '7.62 cm Panzer Abwehr Kanone (PAK) 36(r) or 39(r)' according to which model of Russian gun had been the starting point.

The next upward steps in calibre for the Soviets were to 122 mm (4.8 inches) and 152 mm (6 inches) and in each there were a variety of guns and howitzers. As with many other countries, the Russians had begun in the late 1920s to develop an integrated series of weapons in which a particular carriage would serve for a gun and also for the howitzer of the next upward calibre step. Thus 76 mm guns and 122 mm howitzers, 122 mm guns and 152 mm howitzers were 'partner pieces'. This was a nice and orderly system but it tended to fall apart under the stress of war when it became necessary to improve one particular weapon without reference to its partner. The basic 122 mm howitzer was the Model 1938 and these were taken into German use as the '12.2 cm Haubitze 396(r)' in some numbers. The 122 mm gun had originated in 1931 and was a long-barrelled weapon which could send its 25 kg (55 lb) shell to a range of 20,870 m (10.2 miles) very effectively, but experience showed it to be rather cumbersome due to the long overhanging barrel, and insufficiently flexible in tactical function since its elevation was limited to 45 degrees. In 1937, therefore, it underwent considerable modification; the barrel was arranged so that it could be disconnected from the recoil system and drawn back on to the trail for moving, so as to cut down the vibration of the unsupported barrel, the elevation was altered to allow the gun to reach 65 degrees and thus function, to some extent, as a howitzer, and dual wheels were fitted to improve towing in soft ground. The ballistic performance remained the same. Large numbers of both these weapons were taken by the Germans and put to use against their former owners.

A 152 mm howitzer was placed on the 122 mm gun carriage in 1934, but this underwent the same modification in 1937 so as to improve its flexibility in action and mobility in transport. This was, in fact, a gun-howitzer, a weapon provided with a range of ammunition enabling it to produce high velocity (655 m/sec – 2,150 ft/sec) flat-trajectory fire in the role of a gun, or, with a cartridge system split into twelve charges and the ability to elevate to 65 degrees, lower velocities and high trajectories for firing over intervening crests and thus performing in the howitzer role.

While this was an excellent weapon, it was, in fact, too much of a weapon for many of the tasks it was required to perform, particularly in the howitzer role, and during the war a much lighter 152 mm howitzer, the Model 1943, appeared. This had a smaller propelling charge, with less sub-divisions, and the maximum range was cut from 17,265 m to 12,400 m. However, the weight was also pruned, from 7,128 kg to 3,600 kg, making the Model 43 howitzer a highly mobile weapon.

The initial exuberance of the German advance into Russia was soon curbed when they were confronted with the Soviet T-34 and KV tanks, and this led to a rapid demand for more and better anti-tank guns. The standard issue weapon at that time was the 50 mm PAK 40, while the 88 mm FLAK 18 and 36 anti-aircraft guns were also available as back-up. But there were not sufficient 88 mm guns to provide full protection and the 50 mm gun was marginal in success against these new and well-armoured tanks. This was one reason for the German adaptation of the Soviet 76 mm gun into an anti-tank weapon. Another hurried adaptation was done by taking several hundred old French 75 mm Mle 1897 field guns, removing the barrels and fitting them on to the carriages of the now-obsolescent 50 mm PAK 38 gun. A muzzle brake had to be fitted to the gun in order to reduce the recoil stress delivered to the now over-gunned carriage but even so it became notorious for carriage failures due to over-stress and it was most unstable when fired. Since the muzzle velocity available was no more than 577 m/sec (1,900 ft/sec), a long way below that which was generally thought the optimum for anti-tank shooting, reliance was principally placed in a hollow charge shell which the Germans designed for the gun. Piercing shot, taken from captured Polish Army stocks, and original French high explosive shells were also issued, but the '7.5 cm PAK 97/38' was no more than a hasty stopgap however one looked at it.

The correct answer appeared late in 1941 with the issue of the 7.5 cm PAK 40, a weapon which had been under development since late 1939. In essence it was little more than a scaled-up version of the existing 50 mm gun, but the powerful cartridge was capable of sending a piercing shell which would pierce 102 mm (4 inches) of armour at 1,500 metres range, quite sufficient to deal with any tank then in existence. When provided with a tungsten-cored Arrowhead shot it could pierce 154 mm (6.1 inches) at 500 metres or 115 mm (4.5 in) at 1,500 metres. And when the anti-tank business was slack, it could throw a useful 5.8 kg (13 lb) high explosive shell to 7,680 metres range to double as a field gun.

The 7.5 cm PAK 40 had been designed by Rheinmetall-Borsig; the development contract had been put out to them and also to Krupp, and Krupp now produced their answer to the same specification, the 7.5 cm PAK 41. This was the largest taper-bore weapon to see service; it was, in fact, a 'squeeze-bore' rather than a taper-bore since the diminution of calibre was not constant and gradual throughout the barrel's length but occurred relatively suddenly. The normally-rifled and parallel barrel was 2.95 m long, and to it was screwed a 95 cm tapering section which ended in a short parallel length. Thus the projectile could gather speed up the bore, was then squeezed rapidly down, and had another short stretch in which to become stable again before leaving the

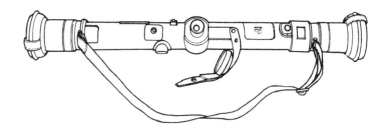

A German short-base rangefinder, using a split-image system, which was issued to all anti-tank gun sections.

muzzle. The projectile weighed 2.59 kg (5.7 lbs) and consisted of the usual tungsten core with collapsible 'skirt' bands of soft steel. The performance was phenomenal: at 500 m range it would pierce 210 mm (8.25 inches) of armour, at 1,000 m 177 mm (6.97 inches) and at 2,000 m, a range at which most anti-tank guns had run out of steam, it could still defeat 124 mm (4.88 inches). Unfortunately, no more than about 150 of these guns were built; tungsten had become a highly critical material in Germany, since all supplies had to be imported, and in 1942 the agonizing decision had to be taken – was tungsten to be used for machine tools or for ammunition? Machine tools won the day, and as the existing tungsten-cored ammunition was used up, so the taper-bore guns went out of service.

At the time that Rheinmetall were developing the 88 mm Flak 41 anti-aircraft gun, the same specification had been given to Krupp, in the usual German manner. Krupp were intent upon developing a 'universal' 88 mm gun which, given suitable carriages, could function as an anti-aircraft, anti-tank or tank gun, and thus their development was slower. Once the Rheinmetall anti-aircraft gun was accepted for service, even with its faults, the Krupp work on that side of the 'universal' design was allowed to slide into the background and they then concentrated on the tank and anti-tank aspect only. Early in 1943 they produced the anti-tank gun, the

8.8 cm PAK 43, and it turned out to have been well worth the waiting. Without resort to taper bores or tungsten-cored shot, the PAK 43 was so powerful that it could put a standard piercing shell through 190 mm (7.5 inches) of armour at 1,000 m range or 159 mm (6.26 inches) at 2,000 metres range. For the carriage, Krupp's moved away from the conventional two-wheeled split trail and adopted a cruciform platform akin to that used with anti-aircraft guns; the gun sat on a low pedestal and when in action the top of the shield was no more than 1.73 m (68 inches) from the ground, making it easy to conceal. For transport two two-wheeled axles could be rapidly attached, and in an emergency the side outriggers could be dropped and the gun fired from its wheels.

Gun barrels are relatively simple things to make; gun carriages, especially one so novel as that of the PAK 43, take longer, and thus there was a delay in providing sufficient of the PAK 43 to the troops in the field in Russia. In order to speed matters along, an extemporized carriage was constructed, using components of various medium and field howitzers, upon which the 88 mm barrel, with a simplified breech mechanism, was fitted. This was a more conventional-looking two-wheeled, split trailed equipment, heavier and more cumbersome to manoeuvre – so much so that the German troops nicknamed it the 'Barndoor' – but its performance was the same as that of the PAK 43 and that was what mattered. At a conference on anti-tank weapons late in 1943 a German captain reported that with a PAK 43/41 (the official name for 'Barndoor') he had knocked out six T-34 tanks in quick succession at a range of 3,500 metres; another report spoke of attacking a T-34 from behind at 600 m range and blowing the engine block some five metres away.

At the same time as the Germans introduced these heavy anti-tank guns, they also introduced some potent tanks, the Panther and Tiger, both of which were extremely well-armed and well-armoured, and this now put the Russians on the defensive. As befitted a country whose ideas on tanks were somewhat in advance of anyone else's, they had started the war with an anti-tank gun rather better than average, a 45 mm (1.77 inch) weapon, still in the usual lightweight mode but somewhat more potent than the usual 37 mm and 40 mm guns. But by 1941 this was stretched to the utmost to deal with the improved German tanks, and when the Panther and Tiger appeared on the scene it was hopelessly outmatched. But by that time they had managed to introduce a better weapon, the 57 mm Model 1941. Although of the same calibre as the British 6 pounder, the Soviet 57 mm was a more potent weapon, its barrel being 73 calibres long rather than the 45 calibres of the British gun. It fired a 3.15 kg (6.9 lb) piercing shell at 1,020 m/sec (3,350 ft/sec) to pierce 140 mm of armour at 500 metres range.

This was good, but it was not good enough to deal with the Tiger tanks with 100 mm of sloped armour on their fronts, except at suicidally short ranges. Fortunately the Soviet 76 mm and 85 mm Divisional field guns were capable of serving as anti-tank guns when necessary; indeed, Soviet artillery employment tended to make little distinction between different types of guns, their view being that if it could shoot, it could shoot at anything. Nevertheless, there was still a place for a heavy anti-tank gun and in 1944 the 100 mm Model 1944 was introduced, firing a 15.6 kg (34.4 lb) piercing shell at 900 m/sec) (2,950 ft/sec) to penetrate 186 mm (7.3 inches) of plate at 500 metres range. This was later improved by adding a tungsten-cored Arrowhead shot which moved at 1,100 m/sec (3,600 ft/sec) to defeat 240 mm (9.4 inches) at the same range.

The Soviets were not the only ones to be confronted with the new and powerful German tanks; the 'Tiger' made its first appearance for British troops in North Africa, but Intelligence had got wind of its coming and the Army were thus able to prepare for it. Not wishing to be caught in the situation which had confronted them over the choice between the 2 pounder and 6 pounder, as early as November

1940 the British Army had begun discussing a future replacement for the 6 pounder. The first proposed solution was an 8 pounder, the barrel of which would be longer but otherwise of the same dimensions as the existing 6 pounder so that it could fit into the same carriages and tank mountings; this, however, would have been so long as to be severely unbalanced in any existing mounting, and cutting it down in order to balance it would have brought the performance down to the level of the 6 pounder, which was no sort of an improvement, so that idea was dropped. After various ballistic solutions had been calculated, the decision was taken to go for a 3 inch (76 mm) gun firing a 17 lb (7.7 kg) shot. The resulting gun was formally approved for service in May 1942 as the 17 pounder; in comparison with the 6 pounder it was a massive weapon, on a heavy split-trail carriage, but it had ample performance and for that the gunners were prepared to put up with the size. But as with the German PAK 43, the provision of barrels soon outstripped the manufacture of carriages, and when the news of the imminent appearance of the Tiger tank in North Africa was received there was a need to do something quickly. In September 1942, therefore, a 17 pounder gun was mounted on to a standard 25 pounder carriage and tested; to most people's surprise, the combination succeeded, a testimonial to the inherent strength of the 25 pounder carriage. Code-named 'Pheasant', these were secretly shipped to North Africa and moved up to the front disguised as 4.5 inch medium guns. They proved to be highly successful, but it is an amusing footnote to the story to relate that, in fact, the first Tiger tanks to be deployed against British troops in the desert were actually stopped and knocked out by well-handled 6 pounders firing from astutely chosen ambush positions.

The 17 pounder was first provided with a plain steel shot which, fired at 2,900 ft/sec (883 m/sec), could defeat 109 mm of plate at 1,000 yards range. Plain steel shot, though, is only at its best when fired against 'homogeneous' armour, that is armour which is of the same consistency and toughness all through. In about 1941, though, the German tanks began appearing with 'face-hardened' plate; as the name implies, this was homogeneous plate which, by a process of carburizing, had the outer face brought to a glass-like hardness. To have made the entire plate so hard would have made it brittle and easy to smash if not pierce, but by confining the hardening to the face the remainder of the plate retained the toughness of homogeneous plate and thus supported the hard face. The effect of this move was to defeat shot by presenting it with an impossibly hard skin.

There was, though, nothing new in all this; the same type of plate had long been used on battleship armour and the answer had been found during the nineteenth century. The answer was to add a cap to the shot, a cap of relatively soft steel which rested on the shoulders of the shot without contacting the point. On striking the armour, this cap disintegrated, but it acted as a shock absorber for the fraction of a second that it held together, taking the initial shock and passing it on to the shoulders instead of the point and then, by devious metallurgical means, acting as a lubricant to assist the shot to pierce the hard skin of the armour; once the skin was pierced, the rest of the plate gave no trouble. And so capped shot appeared on most types of anti-tank gun ammunition from about 1940 onwards. The only disadvantage was that the perfect piercing cap was a poor ballistic shape, and a second cap, of thin steel, but of tapering shape, was fitted over the piercing cap so as to give the complete projectile a less resistant profile as it passed through the air. With this, the 17 pounder could manage 118 mm at 1,000 yards.

But as we have already seen, there comes a time when steel cannot withstand the impact and the designer has recourse to tungsten carbide; we have also discussed the 'composite rigid' or 'Arrowhead' shot and the 'composite non-rigid' shot used with taper and squeeze-bore guns. The basic dichotomy in the design of anti-tank ammunition was that to

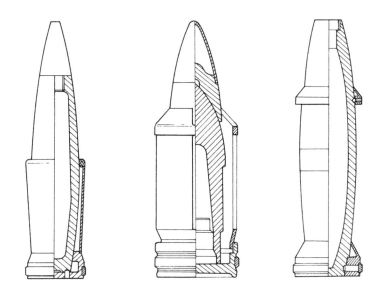

Three German 'sabot' projectiles, showing different methods of designing sabots, all of which would be discarded at the muzzle to allow the basic projectile to continue at high velocity.

obtain the greatest acceleration in the bore and thus the desirable muzzle velocity, the shot should be light in proportion to its cross-section, and yet to retain that velocity in its flight through the air the shot needs to have a high ratio of weight to area. This, indeed, was the reasoning behind the squeeze-bore shot. But to achieve a perfect design without having to resort to some complicated construction of the gun barrel seemed impossible.

In fact the answer had been found by a French ordnance engineer in the early 1930s while looking for the solution to a rather different problem. Edgar Brandt, who is probably best remembered for his contributions to trench mortar design, was trying to find a method of giving field artillery a longer range without having to resort to super-powered cartridges

129

and all the ills that they brought in their train. In essence, his ideal was the same; to have a light projectile in the bore and a heavy one in flight, and he solved it by taking a projectile of a smaller calibre – for example, a 75 mm shell for use in a 105 mm gun – and then building round it a light metal 'sabot' of the bore calibre. By ingenious design it was possible to make this sabot come apart and fall away from the 'subprojectile' after the complete unit had left the gun. So that a light (since most of it was light metal and air-space) 105 mm shell would, immediately after leaving the gun muzzle, turn itself into a normal-weight 75 mm shell, and in effect the 75 mm shell was being propelled at rather better than its normal speed since it had been launched by a 105 mm cartridge. The net result was to endow the 105 mm gun with a much longer range, though, it must be remembered, it was only throwing a 75 mm shell – though to a much greater range than any 75 mm gun could have managed.

Brandt worked on this idea throughout the 1930s and his experiments were fairly well-known throughout the world's military design offices, since he had held demonstrations and published papers about them. In 1940, of course, his work came to an enforced halt, but the torch was taken up elsewhere. In Germany his original idea was pursued, and a number of sabot shells of various types and sizes were produced either to endow signs with longer range or, in several cases, to give anti-aircraft guns a higher velocity and thus a shorter time-of-flight of the shell to the target, a move which would improve their accuracy. In Britain, though, two designers named Permutter and Coppock began, in 1940, to look at Brandt's idea with a view to applying it to a tungsten-cored anti-tank projectile. After experiments using a 25 mm Hotchkiss anti-tank gun and a 2 pounder, by 1942 they had had sufficient success to justify a specification being written for a 6 pounder projectile. This had the tungsten core carried in a streamlined steel sheath and supported in a light alloy four-piece 'sabot' which split in the bore and was discarded outside the gun muzzle, leaving the 'sub-projectile' to travel at 4,050 ft/sec (1,234 m/sec) and pierce an astonishing 146 mm of plate at 1,000 yards range. This 'Armour Piercing, Discarding Sabot' (APDS) shot was approved for service with the 6 pounder in December 1943, by which time Permutter and Coppock had begun working on an enlarged version for the 17 pounder. This appeared in July 1944, had a muzzle velocity of 3,950 ft/sec (1,204 m/sec) and could pierce 231 mm (9.1 inches) at 1,000 yards range, more than enough to see off any tank then in existence.

One might be excused for thinking that with that the anti-tank strength of the British Army was sufficiently well catered for, but while other branches of the British Army (and other services) have frequently been castigated for being slow on the uptake, the gun and ammunition designers have usually been well ahead, when finance allowed them, and they had no intention of being caught out in the future. So in October 1942 a new specification was drawn up, asking for a future anti-tank gun which would show an improvement of at least 25 per cent on the 17 pounder's performance. At that time, of course, the APDS shot was an unknown quantity. The theoretical solution offered by the design experts was a 4.45 inch (113 mm) gun firing a 55 lb (24.9 kg) shot at 2,600 ft/sec (792 m/sec). This '55 pounder' was, in fact, no less than a proposal to take the existing 4.5 inch anti-aircraft gun and turn it into an anti-tank gun, though at that stage of the proceedings, nobody was saying how it was to be done. In March 1943, while this was still being debated, the Ordnance Board pointed out that the projected APDS shot for the 17 pounder would produce better results than this proposed super-gun, and so the idea was quietly dropped.

The next suggestion was, bearing in mind the origin of the 55 pounder, fairly logical; it was a 32 pounder gun derived from the barrel of the 3.7 inch anti-aircraft gun. This promised to have a formidable performance and the idea was approved in September 1943, the weapon to be mounted on a split-trail field carriage and also mounted in a limited-traverse 'tank destroyer' tracked carrier. Development was carried out fairly slowly, since the 17 pounder was perfectly adequate for the time being, and the end of the war arrived before the 32 pounder appeared in the flesh. When it did appear, it was immediately obvious that the days of the 'brute force and ignorance' anti-tank gun were over. The massive equipment weighed over seven tons, was almost as big as a 5.5 inch medium gun, was well-nigh impossible to manhandle in rough country, and, for all its size, barely improved on the 17 pounder's performance. In October 1945 it was sentenced 'not to be perpetuated in service' and after several trials had been carried out, it was made obsolete in 1951. The self-propelled version, known as the 'Tortoise', was a massive 78-ton monster, well armoured and with a useful punch, but too heavy for any existing tank transporter or landing craft; five were built and it, too, was made obsolete.

The Germans had taken a similar road to the British at much the same time and had arrived at a similar destination. Looking for an improvement on the 88 mm guns, a specification was drawn up for a 12.8 cm (5.04 inch) gun, to be developed as a towed anti-tank gun and as a self-propelled tank destroyer. It eventually appeared as the 12.8 cm PAK 44, a formidable weapon; two prototypes were built, by Krupp and by Rheinmetall-Borsig, both using cruciform carriages very similar to that developed for the 8.8 cm PAK 43. The Krupp weapon was moved by two two-wheeled limbers, one at each end, while the Rheinmetall had six wheels, four in a bogie at one end and two on a removable limber at the other; when put into action the limber was removed and the four-wheeled bogie hoisted from the ground but retained on the carriage to add weight and resist recoil. By the time these designs were perfected the war was in its final stages and no more than a handful were made; 51 barrels were made, though, and some were mounted on a variety of captured carriages for experimental purposes. Another 77 were made in slightly different form and used as main armament on the 'Jagdtiger' tank destroyer, a most formidable vehicle.

Although the 12.8 cm PAK 44 was a powerful weapon, the fact remains that it weighed 10 tons and stood about 30 feet long. It could put a 28 kg (62 lb) piercing shell through 230 mm of plate at 1,000 m range, which was probably comparable with the performance of the British 32 pounder, but nevertheless it was far too cumbersome to be considered practical in the anti-tank gun role, a role which demands high mobility and the ability to manhandle the gun into impossible places and conceal it there. Like the dinosaurs of old, the anti-tank gun had grown too big to survive and it was being threatened by a smaller species.

A SEARCH FOR NEW BALLISTICS

The species which replaced the heavy conventional anti-tank gun was the recoilless gun. The idea of developing a gun which dispensed with recoil and thus with the necessity for a heavy and expensive recoil mechanism, and also reduced the need for a heavy trail structure to disperse the recoil blow to the ground and keep the gun stable, had attracted inventors for many years. Some had tried to solve the problem by simply forbidding recoil to happen; clamping the gun securely into some solid and immovable mass, such as a fortress turret or a tank body so that the recoil was driven into the mass and there absorbed by inertia, but there was little point in any of these exercises, since the object behind attaining recoillessness was to save weight, not increase it. An alternative approach was to cancel recoil out, by placing two identical guns back-to-back and firing them simultaneously; the recoil of each would drive into the other and the two would equalize and thus the entire equipment would not move. A progression from this is to make a gun with a single chamber and two barrels, one pointing forward and the other back; one barrel discharges the projectile, the other an equal weight, thus developing recoil in both barrels to cancel each other out. This was perfected into a working gun by Commander Cleland Davis USN during World War I and a number of Davis guns were tried out by the Royal Naval Air Service. There are claims that the Soviet Army used some sort of recoilless guns in the Finnish War of 1939/40 though

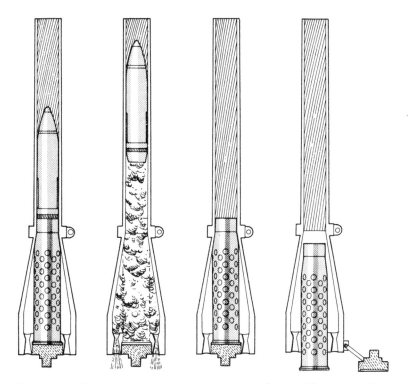

Sequence of events showing the operation of a recoilless gun. On firing, the propellant gases, in addition to pushing the shell from the bore, pass through the holes in the cartridge case and are vented rearwards to develop a counter-recoil thrust.

no details have ever been forthcoming about them. The first major use of this type of weapon came about during the German airborne attack on Crete in 1941.

During the 1930s various German gun designers had been looking at the Davis gun, and the Rheinmetall company developed a very similar weapon for use in aircraft; it was a massive 30 cm (11.8 inch) affair carried underneath a bomber for attacking capital ships, and it obtained its recoillessness by firing a heavy shell from the muzzle and ejecting an equal weight of steel cartridge case from the rear end. Although perfected and tried in flight, this weapon was never actually put to use. But carrying the Davis idea to its logical conclusion, Rheinmetall reasoned that instead of ejecting an equal weight backwards it would be possible to attain the same result by ejecting, say, half the weight at twice the velocity, or a quarter the weight at four times the velocity of the projectile. So long as the product of mass × velocity was the same, recoil was damped out. Taking this to its extreme, if a stream of light gas was ejected at a high enough speed, the gun would still be recoilless.

At its simplest, this can be achieved by simply putting a shell into a gun, packing the chamber with propellant, leaving the breech open and lighting the propellant. The subsequent explosion will eject gas to the rear and eject the shot forward provided sufficient propellant is used; it is theoretically possible, but highly impractical. The German designers reached their goal by placing the propellant into a normal cartridge case which instead of the usual solid brass base had a plastic disc. The breech block had a hole in it which led to a convergent-divergent De Laval nozzle or 'venturi' which accelerated the ejected gas. In some respects it is convenient to think of the result as a gun with a rocket behind it, such that the rocket generates thrust to counteract the recoil; it is not quite true, but as an approximation it will answer. When the German gun was fired the plastic disc resisted just long enough to allow the shell to start moving up the barrel, after which it collapsed and the gas was ejected through the nozzle; the gun did not recoil and thus it could be mounted on nothing more involved than a simple tripod, complete with a pair of tiny wheels for trundling it about.

The first of these guns to enter service with the Luftwaffe

Parachute troops was the 7.5 cm LG 40, 'LG' standing for 'Leicht Geschütz' or 'Light Gun', a non-committal sort of description which was chosen for security reasons. It was a simple equipment which weighed no more than 145 kg (320 lbs) in fighting order and it fired the normal 75 mm 5.8 kg (12.8 lb) high explosive shell to a range of over 7,000 metres, a most impressive performance. It was later furnished with a hollow charge anti-tank shell. It saw use in Crete and would doubtless have seen more use had not the German parachute troops suffered such a bloody nose in that affair as to be virtually disbanded thereafter. A 10.5 cm LG 40 was also produced, firing the standard 14.8 kg (32.6 lb) 105 mm shell to 7,950 metres and weighing only 388 kg (856 lbs). Both these weapons were later used by mountain troops and other units who required lightweight weapons to be carried into difficult terrain.

There were, however, some drawbacks. From the point of view of the higher command echelons, the light gun's appetite for propellant was the principal one. Due to the fact that much of the propellant was converted into gas and blown out through the rearward jet, to obtain the necessary performance from the projectile it was necessary to have a much larger propellant charge than would have been used in the same calibre of conventional gun; in general, it took three times as much powder to propel a shell from a light gun than it did to propel the same shell from a conventional gun. And by 1944 the manufacture of propellant was a critical feature of the German war economy, so much so that the recoilless gun was slowly withdrawn from service and designers were being asked to think up something new.

So far as the soldiers were concerned, the drawback to the recoilless gun was the blast and flame which came out of the rear. There was a danger area behind the gun which stretched to 100 metres, though in fact the danger extended farther than that due to the stones and debris which the blast kicked up. It was impossible to conceal the gun once the first shot had been fired, impossible to hide it in a house, impossible to protect it in a pit, vital to ensure that there was no structure or terrain feature behind it which would bounce the blast and flame back on to the gunners. As one German officer, interrogated after the war, said 'These things were a good deal more popular with their designers than they ever were with their users.'

Britain also developed a series of recoilless guns, though since their development did not begin until the early 1940s, none of the designs reached service before the war ended. Development began in late 1940 when a private experimenter, Sir Dennis Burney, without knowledge of the German work, reached much the same conclusions and designed a gun which would balance recoil by emitting a stream of gas to the rear. His approach was somewhat different in that he adopted a normal cartridge case and drilled a series of large holes in the side walls. The gun was made with an enlarged chamber, such that the perforated cartridge case lay centrally in it; when the gun was fired, gas from the propellant passed through the holes in the case, into the annular space of the chamber and was then directed back to exhaust through a number of venturi jets arranged around the breech.

After various small-calibre experimental weapons, the first design to appeal to the Army was a 3.45 inch (87 mm) weapon which could be fired either from a light tripod or from the shoulder of a resolute man, which, allied with the calibre, led to it being called the '25 pounder shoulder gun'. Other designs followed, including a 3.7 inch (94 mm) suggestion put forward as a possible anti-tank gun, a 95 mm field howitzer with multiple charges, and a 7.2 inch (184 mm) gun which was intended to act as a short-range smasher to defeat the concrete fortifications of Hitler's 'Atlantic Wall'. To achieve this, Sir Dennis had developed a shell of his own design which he called the 'Wallbuster'; a thin-walled projectile, it contained a wire-mesh inner lining packed with plastic explosive and fitted with a fuze at the rear end. On striking the concrete obstacle, the outer casing of the shell peeled away, while the wire-mesh bag of explosive deformed under its own momentum and plastered itself tightly against the concrete, whereupon the base fuze detonated the explosive. The effect was to drive a shattering wave into the concrete, setting up a phenomenon known as the 'Pressure Bar Effect' in which the wave was reflected from the inside face of the concrete and, in doing so, detached a slab from the wall and blew it off at high speed. One or two such shots would rapidly hole any reinforced concrete wall in existence.

In the event, the Burney 'Wallbuster' shell and the 7.2 inch RCL (ReCoilLess) gun were not used in the 1944 invasion; other weapons were available which could do what was needed, and the prospect of a 7.2 inch RCL blasting flame back across the beaches was not viewed with great relish. But after the 'Wallbuster' had been demonstrated in its anti-concrete role, it was suggested that it might be interesting to see what it would do to armour plate, if anything. A trial was set up and the 7.2 inch gun fired against a slab of 6 inch (152 mm) armour; a slab of metal measuring almost two feet square and weighing 117 lbs (53 kg) was blown from the rear face of the plate at high velocity, and a new anti-tank projectile was born.

Although the 7.2 inch 'Wallbuster' undoubtedly did the job, it smacked somewhat of 'overkill' (though nobody in 1944 had yet heard of that phrase) and as a result the 3.7 inch anti-tank RCL was developed to take advantage of the 'Wall-buster'. The 3.45 inch 'shoulder gun' also used one, though it had originally been provided with a hollow charge shell. But due to the time taken to develop these new weapons it was early 1945 before production of service models began and though a number were ready for shipment to Burma, the war ended before they could be got into action. Whereas the Germans had used the RCL as an airborne weapon, the British and Americans were more attracted to it as a method of taking heavy firepower into the jungle, along trails which would not permit the towing of conventional guns.

Burney's last designs were for an 8 inch long-range recoilless gun, which proved to be a failure, and for a 4.7 inch RCL anti-tank gun. In 1944 development work was put in hand by a Government establishment, and after the war they took up the 4.7 inch where Burney left off. They also did a great deal of fundamental research on the 'Wallbuster' shell, and from it developed a serviceable projectile which could be used in conventional as well as RCL guns; this became known as the 'High Explosive, Squash-Head' (HESH) shell in British service and as the 'High Explosive, Plastic' (HE-P) in American usage. The 4.7 inch gun eventually turned into the 120 mm Battalion Anti-Tank Gun (BAT) and came into service in the early 1950s; whilst still a recoilless design, it had abandoned Burney's perforated cartridge case in favour of a plastic-based case which more resembled some of the early German designs.

American development of RCL guns began when a German 105 mm LG42 was captured and shipped back to the USA in 1943. A simple copy of this was made, called the 105 mm Howitzer RCL T9, which fired the normal American 105 mm howitzer shell. In order to reduce the internal pressures, the driving band of the shell was pre-cut to match the rifling of the gun, a process which demanded some precision on the part of the loader. The initial trial of this gun was quite entertaining; the first propelling charge was 25 ounces (710 gm) of powder, on the principle of starting with something safe and working upwards. The first shot was fired, with the result that the shell remained firmly in place inside the gun while the whole equipment 'recoiled' forward five inches. After this auspicious start the charge was gradually increased and eventually the gun performed quite well – with a charge weighing eight pounds (3.6 kg).

The T9 howitzer had been developed by the Artillery Section of the Research & Development Service; at the same time, the Infantry Section began work on a design of their own, which would appear to have been influenced by the Burney designs. It used a perforated cartridge case, though one with many more smaller perforations, and also adopted the idea of pre-engraving the shell driving band. The first model was a 57 mm (2.24 inch) 'Recoilless rifle T15' which, like the Burney 3.45 inch, could be fired from the shoulder or from a modified machine-gun tripod. It proved to be successful in a series of tests and by early 1945 over 2,000 guns were ordered and almost a million rounds of ammunition. Both high explosive and hollow charge shells were developed, and the first supplies were ready in time to be sent to troops in both Europe and the Pacific before the war ended. In Germany, the US 17th Airborne Division used them in the region of Essen, whilst in the Pacific they were first used in Okinawa in June.

Once the 57 mm model had been approved, work began on a 75 mm version, more or less a simple scale-up from the smaller gun. As with the 57 mm, it was approved early in 1945 and small numbers were sent, with the 57 mm weapons, for practical evaluation in the hands of troops. The ammunition was produced relatively easily by taking the existing high explosive, hollow charge and white phosphorus shells used with the standard 75 mm Pack Howitzer and simply pre-engraving the driving bands.

The Infantry Section R & D then went on to develop a 105 mm gun along similar lines and the pilot model was tested in comparison to the T9 RCL howitzer. The result was a clear-cut decision in favour of the Infantry Section's model, which was known as the 'Kromuskit' design from the names of the two principal designers, Kroger and Musser. Procurement of no less than 5,000 105 mm RCL guns was authorized in July 1945, but the end of the war came before production could get under way and this was immediately pruned to fifty and then cancelled completely. As with the British development work, the end of the war gave the researchers a chance to drop plans for immediate production in favour of sitting back to do some basic research instead of simply rushing into business with the first thing that worked. The 105 mm eventually appeared in about 1950, to see service in Korea, but it was not a success and had to be withdrawn and re-designed.

The Western Allies continued in their wartime development of the RCL gun because they could afford to do so; the Germans, as we have said, abandoned their work in this line because it was absorbing far too much of their propellant resources. But abandoning a solution does not make the problem go away, and the German Army were still looking for a lightweight anti-tank gun. In late 1943, therefore, they approached various manufacturers asking for a weapon which would fire a hollow charge projectile with sufficient accuracy to guarantee hitting a one metre square target at 750 metres range and, withal, use less propellant than either a recoilless gun or a rocket in doing so. Rheinmetall-Borsig had been experimenting with a completely new ballistic idea for some time, and they now adopted this and produced a workable weapon known as the '8 cm Panzer Abwehr Werfer 8H63'. The system used became known as the 'High–Low Pressure System' and it was a remarkable breakthrough.

The problem, it will be remembered, was to devise a weapon which was light in weight and which used as little propellant as possible. The High-Low Pressure gun had a very light barrel but a fairly substantial breech and chamber. The projectile was based on an existing 8 cm mortar bomb, fin-stabilized and streamlined, converted internally to become a hollow-charge missile. The cartridge case used was the standard case long in service with the 105 mm leFH 18 field howitzer; thus the basic components were items which were in ready supply and of proved serviceability. In the mouth of the cartridge case was placed a heavy steel disc pierced with eight venturi holes, and the tail of the projectile was anchored to this plate by a shearable pin. Inside the case was a charge of 360 gm (12.7 ounces) of powder.

When this round was loaded, the bomb lay in the smooth-bored barrel of the gun, while the heavy steel plate in the mouth of the cartridge was butted against a step in the front end of the chamber, so that it could not move forward. When the charge was fired, it exploded inside the case and developed therein a pressure of about 1100 kg/cm^2 (6 tons-/in^2) and this high-pressure gas was leaked through the venturis in the plate and into the space behind the projectile. Due to its passage through the vents in the plate, the pressure build-up in the actual chamber of the gun was relatively slow, and when it reached about 550 kg/cm^2 (3 tons/in^2) the shearable pin gave way and the projectile was projected up the bore and off to the target. Thus the high pressure of the explosion was confined within the heavy breech unit, whilst the pressure in the barrel which actually sent the bomb on its way was restricted to half the chamber value.

The 8 cm P A W 8H63 proved to be a great success; the first carriage designed for it was insufficiently robust and had to be strengthened; and in fact a large number were actually mounted on old 5 cm PAK 38 anti-tank gun carriages which were available. Some 200 guns were built between November 1944 and March 1945 and they proved to be most effective, the bomb being capable of piercing 140 mm (5.5 inches) of plate. A 105 mm version, to be known as the 10 cm 10H64, was under development by Krupp as the war ended.

Strangely, although the system was examined very thoroughly by ballistic experts of various countries in the post-war years, very little use has been made of the idea since then. It has been used in a Naval anti-submarine mortar in British service, in a shoulder-fired 40 mm grenade launcher by the Americans, and in a light tank gun by the Swiss. In more recent years it has re-appeared in a 73 mm gun mounted in the Soviet Mechanized Infantry Combat Vehicle BMP-1.

THE SEARCH FOR LONGER RANGE

World War II turned into a war of great mobility, a fact which militated against the use of 'artillery of position' unless it was powerful enough to be able to command a considerable area and thus avoid having to move whenever the front line fluctuated. The British Army had gone to France in 1939 taking with it such World War I veterans as their 9.2 inch (234 mm) and 12 inch (305 mm) howitzers, weapons which had been designed to be put down behind a static front where they could pound away for weeks before finding it necessary to move. Moving them was a major operation; the 9.2 inch howitzer was transported in four loads behind heavy tractors and assembled with the aid of cranes and slings, a process taking a day or more. In order to keep the platform as compact as possible for transportation, it was curtailed to such a degree that the entire mounting tended to jump into the air when it fired, and the only cure for this was the addition of the 'earth box', a massive iron box built at the front of the mounting and then shovelled full of earth, no less than eleven tons (11,175 kg) of it before fire could be opened. And, of course, when the time came to move, the first task was to shovel the eleven tons of earth out of the box again. The 12 inch howitzer, built on similar lines, was, naturally, bigger, and required 20 tons of earth in the box. It travelled in six loads, all drawn by caterpillar tractors, and went down in history under the soldiers' name of 'The 12 inch Roadhog'.

As might be expected, in the withdrawal to Dunkirk in

1940 these monsters were abandoned, and the British were astute enough to realize that there was no profit to be had in perpetuating the design; those which remained in England were deployed around the south coast as anti-invasion weapons, but apart from that they played no further part in the war. A comparable weapon was the 18 inch (457 mm) railway howitzer which had been built just too late for use in World War I. Had the campaign remained in France, then doubtless this weapon would have been shipped there, but before that could happen the need no longer arose. It, too, found its way to the south-eastern corner of England, there to be photographed for propaganda purposes and billed as a fearsome cross-channel monster to threaten the guns which the Germans were then massing on the French coast. But the truth was that the 18 inch with its 2,500 lb (1,133 kg) shell had a maximum range of no more than 22,300 yards and could no more cross the channel with its fire than it could fly.

The Germans had owned a number of similarly cumbersome equipments in 1918, but the post-war restrictions had swept them into the scrapyards – except one 420 mm (16.5 inch) howitzer which managed to remain in an experimental firing ground and was periodically called upon to fire tests of experimental shells – and in the early 1930s the designers had got to work to produce weapons which were more capable of rapid movement in support of a high-speed war.

In 1935 Rheinmetall began development of a 24 cm (9.45 inch) gun known simply as the 'Kanone 3', an outstanding technical achievement. It was a conventional type of gun, capable of firing a 151 kg (333 lb) shell to a range of 37.5 km (23.3 miles), but to do this it had to be a substantial weapon, weighing all of 54,800 kg (54 tons) in the firing position. To move this mass, it had to be dismantled and carried on special trailers in six loads, one of which was an electric generator set to provide power for assembling the weapon and operating the elevation gears. The basic portion of the mounting was a box with a four-wheeled bogie at one end and a two-wheeled limber at the other, the limber being removed to go into action. This was placed on top of two ground platforms, being pivoted on the front one and geared so as to move the rear of the basic structure across the rear platform so as to point the gun as required. On top of the basic structure was a top carriage, connected by means of an hydro-pneumatic recoil system. Into this top carriage went the gun, in a conventional cradle with another recoil system interposed between the cradle and the gun. Thus when the gun fired it recoiled in the cradle, and at the same time the top carriage recoiled across the basic structure. This dual recoil system soaked up the recoil force so well that the entire mounting was a good deal lighter than would have had to be the case with a normal single recoil system.

Six 'Kanone 3' were built and issued in 1938, but they were the only ones. The Army, while admitting that it was a technical *tour de force*, complained that the performance was incommensurate with the size of the weapon and the amount of work necessary to bring it into action. A new specification was drawn up, asking for a weapon with a range of about 50 km and capable of moving in a single unit. This latter requirement was patently impossible and was later amended to permit two loads, whereupon Krupp set about building the 'Kanone 4'. Unfortunately, the experimental design was severely damaged in an air raid on Essen, and the project was then abandoned.

The dual recoil system, though, had taken various people's fancy, and Krupp used it in their design of a heavy howitzer, the 21 cm Mörser 18, developed in 1939. This was lighter and more portable than the Kanone 3, moving in two loads, mounting and barrel. The adoption of dual recoil again allowed a reduction in weight and in action and the 21 cm Mörser 18 weighed only 16,700 kg (16.4 tons); it fired a 113 kg (250 lb) shell to a range of 16,700 metres. To go with this, a 'partner piece' was developed, the 17 cm Kanone 18, and these two became the mainstay of German heavy Artillery. The 17 cm gun fitted on to the same mounting as the 21 cm howitzer and fired a 62 kg (138 lb) shell to a range of 29,600 metres.

Assuming that such a gun was in a location which allowed it to fire over an arc of 90 degrees, this means that it was capable of putting a shell anywhere in an area of some 688 square kilometres, which is a useful area of command for a single weapon. Even so, the German Army were anxious to improve this, and as a result a number of projects were inaugurated to try and extend the range of artillery weapons; not merely the 17 cm and 21 cm pieces but all weapons came under this review, and some quite remarkable solutions appeared.

The basic method of obtaining more range from a gun is, of course, to use a bigger cartridge, but there are practical limits to this; most guns, in their standard form, use the largest and most powerful propelling charge possible within the bounds of safety and longevity, and increasing the charge will merely wear the gun out at an uneconomical speed or stress it beyond safe limits. Another way is to make the barrel longer, but again, there are practical limits to this and a worthwhile improvement is only obtained by excessive length. The sabot solution, which we have already discussed, gives an increase in range at the expense of the size of shell, but this trade-off is frequently acceptable, especially in large calibres; the difference, at the receiving end, between say a 20 cm shell and a 24 cm shell is not likely to be remarked upon by the recipient. Many sabot designs were tested by the German Army but none were in regular service by the time the war ended.

Another attractive idea is to build a rocket into the shell and ignite it somewhere along the trajectory so as to give the shell an additional thrust. The first such shell to be introduced for service, though on a limited scale and more in the nature of an extended trial, was for the 15 cm heavy field howitzer 18. The shell was first issued in late 1941, on the Eastern Front, and contemporary reports speak of the voluminous operating instructions and safety regulations which accompanied it, none of which were calculated to inspire confidence in the new projectile. The lower half of the shell contained a rocket motor which used solid propellant, while the forward half contained the payload and fuze. The normal shell for this weapon weighed 43 kg (95 lbs) and ranged to 13,250 metres; the rocket-assisted shell weighed 45 kg (100 lbs) and ranged to 19,000 metres, a worthwhile improvement.

The next weapon to be selected for rocket assistance was a railway gun, one of the finest designs to come from any country during this century. The '28 cm Kanone 5 in Eisenbahnlafette' (11 inch Gun 5 on railway mounting) had begun its development in 1934, entered service in 1936 and was thereafter in constant production until the war ended, some 28 being built. Much of the research from the super-long-range K 12 was used in the design, and it had a barrel rifled with twelve deep grooves to fire shells fitted with twelve splines on the sidewalls. This standard shell weighed 255.5 kg (563.4 lbs) and produced a muzzle velocity of 1,128 m/sec (3,700 ft/sec) to reach a range of 62 km (38.6 miles). One of these guns became notorious as 'Anzio Annie', bombarding the invasion beaches at Anzio and making life miserable for the invaders throughout that phase of the campaign; it was eventually captured at Civitavecchia and shipped back to America, where it is today on exhibition at the Aberdeen Proving Ground Museum.

The rocket-assisted shell developed for this gun was of novel construction; the rocket motor was in the head of the shell and the payload was in the rear section. The blast pipe of the rocket passed down the centre of the shell, in the middle of the payload, and thus had to be carefully insulated so as not to ignite the high explosive. A time fuze in the nose was the igniter for the rocket motor; the payload was detonated by impact fuzes carried within the shell. The time fuze was set,

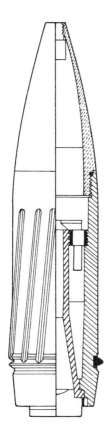

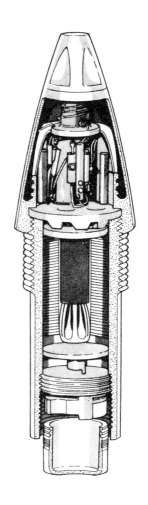

A German rocket-assisted shell for the 28 cm Railway Gun K5. The forward section carries the rocket motor, ignited by a time fuze after 19 seconds of flight. The explosive payload is packed around the rocket blast pipe in the rear section.

The Proximity Fuze. On firing the electrolyte ampoule breaks, activating the battery and radio units.

before firing, to run for 19 seconds; at the end of that time the shell was just approaching the highest point of its trajectory and the rocket motor was ignited so that the upward 'leg' of the trajectory was extended beyond the normal point, thus increasing the range. The shell weighed very slightly less than the standard shell, had almost the same muzzle velocity, but had a maximum range of 86.5 km (53.75 miles) an increase of 24.3 km or about 38 per cent.

This was very welcome, but there was, unfortunately, a drawback. All gun shells which are spin-stabilized tend to develop a motion around their trajectory called 'yaw'; the shell's centre of gravity follows the trajectory, but the nose will deviate in a slow spiral. This usually settles down after the highest point on the trajectory has been passed and the shell becomes stable. But if the shell was yawing off its trajectory at the instant the rocket motor generated thrust, then the shell was given a boost not along the trajectory but slightly off to one side; it might be yawing 'up' and so would gain a little range, or yawing 'down' and thus lose a little. Or it might be yawing to one side or the other and thus deviate from the predicted course. The net result of this was that the normal 'zone' of the gun, into which the shell must, by the laws of probability, fall was considerably extended. In the case of the 28 cm K5(E) shell the zone at the target was a rectangle some 3.4 km long by 200 metres wide, so that the accuracy with rocket assistance was far below that obtained by a normal shell.

Although experimenters continued to work on rocket-assisted shells in Germany during the war, no others were put into service. Instead, a new approach was tried, again on the 28 cm K5(E) gun. During the 1930s the Army had built a secret experimental establishment at Peenemunde, on the Baltic, in which the famous V-1 and V-2 missiles were developed; in Peenemunde was a highly advanced wind tunnel, and when work on the missiles was not being performed, this tunnel was made available to other branches of the Army

150

Weapons Office, and there an Engineer Giessner developed a fin-stabilized projectile which came to be called the 'Peenemunde Pfeil Geschoss' or Peenemunde Arrow Shell. It was a long, slender projectile of excellent ballistic shape and with four large fins at its tail end. Around the centre was a discarding sabot, since the body of the shell was much less in diameter than the bore of the proposed weapon, and when in the gun the shell rested on this sabot and on the tips of the four fins. The sabot also acted as a gas-check, so that the propellant gases pushed against it and thus transferred the thrust to the centre section of the projectile, half pushing and half pulling the shell out of the bore.

The PPG shell developed for the 28 cm K5(E) required some changes in the gun, since the great virtue of a fin-stabilized shell was that it required no rifling and the gun could be a smoothbore. For various reasons, 31 cm (12.2 inches) was selected as the calibre for the smooth barrel and this was duly fitted to one gun for test. The shell weighed 136 kg (300 lbs) and was 1.911 m (75.2 inches) long, with the body of 120 mm (4.7 in) diameter. On firing, it left the bore at 1,525 m/sec (5,000 ft/sec), discarded its central sabot as it left the muzzle, and flew to a maximum range of 151 km (93.8 miles), the longest range ever achieved by a service artillery weapon. Two of these smoothbore weapons, known as the '28 cm K5 (E) Glatt' were eventually built, and one of them was actually employed against the advancing US Third Army in 1945 at a range of about 70 miles.

The arrow shell, with its high velocity and added range, was an attractive proposition for anti-aircraft use, since the improved velocity would reduce the time of flight of the shell to a given height, thus improving the chances of success, since the aircraft would have had less chance to move away from the estimated point of impact. The additional range would also, of course, improve the ceiling of the gun and thus allow it to threaten a deeper belt of sky. As a result much work was done in developing a suitable PPG shell for the

105 mm FLAK 39 gun and several specimens were developed. The work was not completed before the end of the war, so we do not know what performance was obtained, but it is known that the inventors were having second thoughts on the matter; whilst the PPG was undoubtedly an efficient projectile, the fact remained that it demanded extremely careful manufacture of high-grade materials. This was acceptable in a large-calibre railway gun which might fire ten or a dozen rounds a day at a distant target, but it was not a feasible proposition, in the Germany of 1944–45, for a gun which, by its very nature, demanded hundreds of shells for a single night's employment against enemy aircraft. Even if a suitable shell had been perfected, it is unlikely that it would have been put into service in this weapon.

We cannot leave the subject of ultra-long-range weapons without stopping to consider the most outlandish design of all, the remarkable device which masqueraded under several titles, among them 'The Millipede', 'Busy Lizzie' and 'Vergaltungswaffen Drei' (Vengeance Weapon 3 or V-3), though its more formal name was the '15 cm Hochdruckpumpe' or 'High Pressure Pump', a piece of terminology deliberately vague in the interests of secrecy.

The HDP was the brain-child of an engineer named Conders, who worked for the Röchling Iron & Steel Works of Saarbrücken. His idea was to build an enormously long gun barrel and then add auxiliary breeches and chambers to it, herringbone fashion, at intervals along the bore. The shell would be launched into the barrel by a cartridge in the conventional manner, and as it passed the auxiliary chambers, charges in them would be fired in succession, thus adding gas and boosting the projectile to an extremely high velocity before it finally left the muzzle. In this manner the shell would be given a range which he calculated as something in the order of 150 kilometres or more. Whether or not Conders knew it, the idea was actually as old as breech-loading ordnance, having been tried at various times and with varying degrees of failure since the 1880s; indeed, at almost the same time as Conders was making his calculations the same idea was being put forward to the Ordnance Board in Britain. The Board, however, wasted no time in throwing the proposition out.

The Rochling company had been responsible for the development of a special anti-concrete shell, a long projectile with stabilizing fins which sprang out into the airstream to give additional stability, since spinning was insufficient with such a long shell. Conders adapted this shell to his HDP design and built a 20 mm calibre model gun which appeared to work well and prove his theories. He then managed to obtain the ear of Hitler, who was always open to grandiose ideas, and an enormous fifty-barrel complex of HDP guns was planned to be built into a French hillside, aligned upon London, to fire a constant barrage of 15 cm shells at that ample target.

We have here no place for the long saga of experiment and disaster which followed the development of the HDP. Suffice it to say that the experimental guns blew up in various ways, the shells flew erratically, and the monster gun emplacement in France was bombed into rubble, partially rebuilt and then finally captured by advancing Allied troops after the invasion of Europe. Two scaled-down models of the HDP were eventually deployed, laid out on a hillside and fired in support of the Ardennes Offensive in December 1944, but they were then blown up as the German troops were pushed back and all records of the weapon's performance (or lack of it) were destroyed.

The basic and unsolvable defect in the Conders weapon was that it was impossible to time the ignition of the auxiliary chambers with sufficient precision, so that the boosting thrust was never delivered in a regular manner. There is no record of how much money, energy and time were sunk into this vast folly but it remains in the memory to serve as an object lesson that optimistic inventors, particularly in the weapons field, must always be subject to the sobering influence of technical experts.

*   *   *

Although they form a subject on their own, it should be borne in mind that one of the major areas of technical advance in artillery during World War II was that of the self-propelled gun. Broadly speaking, there were two avenues of approach to self-propulsion of artillery, two avenues well exemplified by the German and Soviet technique on the one hand and the British and American on the other, although there were exceptions to the general rule on both sides. The Germans and Soviets regarded the self-propelled gun as a second-class tank, a direct-fire weapon mounted in a well-protected armoured casing carried on tracks, which would accompany the infantry in their advance and deal immediately with any obstacle which appeared. As an off-shoot of this they perfected the 'tank destroyer' vehicle, again a well-armoured tracked chassis carrying as heavy and high-velocity a gun as could be managed, designed for the sole purpose of roving the front and seeking out enemy tanks to destroy with its superior firepower. Intriguing and effective as these assault guns and tank destroyers might be, they can scarcely be regarded as artillery.

The other point of view was simply to regard the self-propelled gun as a normal field or divisional artillery weapon which was endowed with tracks so that the artillery support unit was capable of the same degree of cross-country mobility as the armoured units it was supporting, and this was the aspect which received most attention in Britain and the USA. The American 105 mm howitzer and the British 25 pounder were both mounted into self-propelled chassis derived from standard tank components, but far from being strongly armoured their protection was minimal and the carriages were open-topped structures. The guns were organized and deployed in precisely the same fashion as their towed equivalents, engaging in indirect supporting fire and being assimilated into the overall artillery command structures. The only way in which they differed from towed batteries was simply that they were self-sufficient, required no tractors, were slightly quicker to occupy or leave a location, and found cross-country movement quicker and easier.

As we have said, there were exceptions to the general rule. The German infantry owned a number of guns of their own, which they operated as immediate support weapons and which were not part of the divisional artillery organization. These included a number of 75 mm light cannon and, at the top of the scale, a simple and robust 15 cm known as the 'sIG' for 'schwere Infanterie Geschütz'. In 1940 a number of these were mounted in simple armoured boxes on top of Panzer I and II chassis, but in most cases they were used in direct-fire supporting roles, rumbling along behind the advancing infantry. The only major German SP gun which acted other than as an assault gun and which paralleled the Allied 105 mm and 25 pounder, was the fitting of the standard 105 mm leFH18 into a highly modified Panzer II chassis; this became known as the 'Wespe' (Wasp) and over 600 were built in 1943 and 1944.

A similar exception was the American embracement of the 'tank destroyer' idea, one which they pursued throughout the war with great tenacity, though with rather less success since they never really had a good enough gun for the task they set themselves. Moreover the tank destroyer crews tended to take the bit between their teeth and go roving off looking for trouble and pretending they were tanks. But again, this was not artillery in the pure sense of the word.

Where American mechanical expertise showed itself best was in their application of the self-propelled idea to medium and heavy artillery well in advance of any other nation. In fact, the first American self-propelled gun was the elderly 155 mm M1917 (the French GPF gun) placed on top of a chassis derived from the M3 Lee tank, the design of which

155

was completed in June 1941. Having built 100 of these, the Army suddenly had an attack of cold feet and decided there was no place for them in the service; they were put away in store and it was not until early in 1944 that someone realized that a self-propelled medium gun might be a desirable piece of equipment in the forthcoming invasion of Europe. The guns were taken from store, refurbished and issued, and subsequently served very successfully, so much so that more interest was taken in the idea of large self-propelled weapons. The Ordnance Department, responsible for design, had not been deterred by the Army's lack of interest and had spent the intervening time in perfecting other designs which, once interest was aroused, they were quick to display. Eventually self-propelled versions of the 155 mm Gun M1, the 155 mm Howitzer M1, the 8 inch Howitzer M1, the 8 inch Gun M1 and the 240 mm Howitzer M1 were all developed, though the latter two were never adopted for service.

* * *

At 3.30 am on 13 June 1944 the guided missile era was ushered in as ten V-1 pilotless bombs were launched from sites in France against London. Five crashed almost immediately, one sailed off into the darkness never to be heard of again, and the remaining four managed to reach England and land in various parts of the Home Counties. This came as no surprise to the British defences who had been forewarned of the threat, but since the technical details of the missile were not known to them, the actual matter of countering this new form of attack proved to be difficult. Plans had been drawn up late in 1943 to deploy guns and fighter aircraft round London, but the move of troops to the continent for the invasion had depleted the available forces and when the flying bomb attacks began London was defended by a ring of 138 heavy and 246 light anti-aircraft guns. As the attack increased, so the numbers of guns were augmented by extra weapons lifted from their locations elsewhere in Britain and hurriedly redeployed close to London. Fighter aircraft patrolled the coast and over Kent, acting as a first defensive line, after which the guns took over, with a backstop of barrage balloons to catch what was left. Even so, far too many of the bombs were evading all the defences and landing in the London area and eventually the guns were redeployed along the south-eastern coast. The fighter aircraft then had the area of the Channel in which to act, plus the area behind the guns, and in this way the results were vastly improved.

At first sight, the flying bomb should have been stopped dead in its tracks by anti-aircraft fire since it was, after all, the perfect target. It flew at a constant height and speed in a perfectly straight line without dodging or jinking, the very sort of target which all anti-aircraft fire control systems were designed to cater for. But the flying bomb had been carefully designed by people who knew all about anti-aircraft guns and their capabilities and it had been designed so that it flew at the worst possible combination of speed and height. It moved at 350–400 mph (560–640 km/hr) and at about 3,500 feet (1,065 m) altitude; it was at the limits of height for the light guns and it was too low for the heavy guns since they had to make fast angular movements in order to keep up with the target. And since the range was changing very rapidly, the calculation and setting of the time fuzes on the shells was erratic.

It sometimes happens, though, that technical development bears fruit just in time to defeat a specific threat which was never envisaged when the development began, and this was to be the case in the flying bomb battle, when a number of lines of research all came together to form the perfect defensive system. In the first place, radar had been undergoing steady improvement throughout the war years and had now reached a point where it was possible for a radar set to be 'locked' on to a target and then follow it without human intervention, following smoothly and accurately and with a better degree of consistency than could be achieved by a human operator. Secondly, electrical predictors, which calculated the future position of the target and deduced gun data to hit it, had been improved and were now capable of delivering outputs which could directly control the pointing of the gun. This was achieved by the third component, the development of power-actuated gun mountings in which elevation and traverse were performed by electric or hydraulic motors which responded to the small electrical signals from the predictors. All these things led to a situation in which the target could be smoothly tracked, the information sent to the predictor, and the predictor could then point the gun without any human intervention along the line. All that was needed was to solve the fuze problem so as to guarantee bursting the shell at the appropriate point on the trajectory, and this was solved by the development of the proximity fuze.

The proximity fuze was another dream which had been around for several years, waiting for technology to catch up with it. The idea was to have a fuze which, instead of relying on an estimate of the target's position and the time of the shell's flight to meet it, would directly sense the fact that the shell was close to the target and then detonate it automatically. The first such fuze to reach service was developed in Britain in 1940 and used with anti-aircraft rockets; it was a sizeable piece of apparatus, far too big to be used with a gun shell and far too sensitive to withstand being fired from a gun. This first fuze, known confusingly as the 'Pistol No. 710', operated on a photo-electric system; it carried a series of PE cells which 'looked' outwards through windows in the fuze body and which were 'tuned' to normal daylight. When the shadow of the aircraft fell across the window, this was sensed by the PE cell which then, by an electrical circuit, detonated the warhead of the rocket. They were moderately effective, though sensitive to such things as clouds and birds, and were completely non-effective against aircraft which flew at night.

When the early radar scientists began developing gun-directing radars for anti-aircraft fire they were somewhat upset to find that their best efforts at accuracy were being sabotaged by the error inherent in the use of time fuzes. Their first reaction was to try and develop a fuze which would detect the reflected radar signal from the target and use this to trigger off the detonation. This was theoretically possible, but it demanded more receiving equipment than could be packed into the extremely confined space in the nose of the shell. The next idea was to develop a tiny radio transmitter and receiver unit which would fit into the normal contours of a fuze, and have this transmit a signal as it went through the air. By arranging the antennae, it was possible to make the zone of radio emission the same as the lethal zone of the shell, so that if the radio signal struck a target and reflected from it to trigger the detonation, the target was in the right place to receive the subsequent benefit.

But England in 1940 had no facilities for putting such a device into production, and there was a great deal of basic development still required on the idea; such things as miniature valves, condensers, resistors, and, most of all, a reliable battery which would sit in store for an indefinite period without deteriorating, and then, in a split second, suddenly come to life when the fuze was fired and begin delivering large amounts of electricity.

In 1941 the Tizard Commission went to the United States to reveal British advances in electronic technology and offer various devices to the Americans. The US Navy took up the development of the proximity fuze and by the middle of 1943 were using it with their fleet anti-aircraft guns in the Pacific. Designs suitable for army weapons were then worked out (since, due to various electrical reasons, the fuze had to be matched to the projectile and gun) and by the middle of 1944 a fuze suited to the British 3.7 inch and American 90 mm guns was in production. These fuzes were now brought into use against the flying bomb, and the combination of all these various technical developments, at the right time and in the right place, resulted in a 'kill rate' attributable to anti-aircraft fire as high as 82 per cent.

The proximity fuze was later applied to ground fire. It had long been appreciated that the only way to inflict casualties upon enemy troops concealed behind cover or in trenches was to burst the high explosive shell in the air above, so that fragments of the shell were driven downwards to overcome the protection. This could be done in two ways, by 'time fire' or 'ricochet fire'. Time fire required the use of a time fuze, operating either by the burning of a length of carefully selected and graded gunpowder or by the functioning of a clockwork mechanism. In either case it was unlikely that the first estimate of the fuze timing would be correct, and thus it was the practice to adjust the fuze for a few shots until the shells were bursting in the right place, then fire 'for effect' the necessary rounds required to deal with the target. Not surprisingly, the first burst of a time fuze in the air sent the enemy looking for protection, and by the time the 'fire for effect' arrived, he was out of harm's way. Ricochet fire demanded a special type of impact fuze, one which would function on a glancing impact with the ground but which would not detonate the shell until a small delay had taken place, usually something in the order of 0.15 of a second. With such a fuze, the gunner fired at a low elevation so that the shell struck the ground in front of the target area and ricocheted upward as the delay took place, so that, if he had got it just right, the delay would run out and detonate the shell just as it passed over the enemy trench. The French and American armies were keen on this practice, but it was rarely employed by the British, largely because of their equipments. The French 75 mm gun lent itself to this system since it used a relatively high velocity and a low trajectory; the British 18 pounder and 25 pounder were of lower velocity and had a trajectory which, at average ranges, brought the shell in too steeply to bounce.

The advent of the proximity fuze, though, promised to end

both these systems; since the fuze automatically measured the distance to the target and detonated itself at the optimum lethal range, there was no need to make any calculations or trial shots. One simply fired the fuzed shell into the area and left the fuze to work it all out. The only drawback which appeared in practice was that different types of terrain gave different degrees of reflection to the fuze signal; thus snow or water-logged ground caused the shell to burst high due to the better reflectivity for the radio signal, whilst firing into woods or forests usually meant that the fuzes took their reflection from the tops of the trees and, again, burst too high.

In the anti-aircraft field the proximity fuze provided another advantage in so far as it did not require to be set, and thus the mechanically complex automatic fuze-setter/rammer devices were no longer required. Cutting out one of the preparatory steps to loading also speeded up the rate of fire, and it also suggested that it might be possible to develop auto-loading guns with a very high rate of fire. Work on these was beginning as the war came to an end.

ARTILLERY IN PEACETIME

The end of the war in Europe revealed an incredible number of guided missile projects under way in Germany, missiles for anti-aircraft fire, for land bombardment, even for firing at tanks. The end of the war in Japan disclosed the presence of the nuclear bomb. The combination of these two technical achievements was seized upon by the public as meaning the end of conventional warfare, and no small number of soldiers and politicians were stampeded into the same sort of opinion. The immediate response to the war, in the Western nations at least, was the inevitable running-down of military forces and cancellation of scores of development and production contracts. Such money and effort as became available for military equipment development was largely spent on the new field of missiles, but it was soon apparent that these were going to be slow in reaching perfection and that, for the time being, conventional artillery would still be needed. Much of this, would, of course, come from the vast stocks of guns accumulated during the war and in that respect the situation was very much as it had been in 1919. But at the same time, developments in other weapons fields made sure that artillery design could not stand entirely still; for example the jet aircraft had appeared on the scene during the closing months of the war, and it was soon obvious that aircraft speeds were about to be multiplied by a considerable factor. And if the wartime guns had been stretched to fire at a flying bomb moving at 350 mph, what chance did they stand against a jet aircraft moving at twice that speed?

The fight against the flying bomb had demonstrated that power-operated guns could be built to keep up with the speed of the aircraft; the problem was to get a worthwhile number of shots off while it was within range. The Americans had been the first to move on this idea when in late 1944 they began development of a new 75 mm anti-aircraft gun, the calibre having been chosen as being the smallest which could accept a proximity fuze and still carry a worthwhile payload of explosive in the shell. This was an ambitious project, since the gun was to carry its own radar and fire control computer actually on the mounting. To achieve a fast rate of fire, two revolver-type magazines were fitted behind the gun, feeding alternately into a central rammer. Development was slow, since the first gun designed failed to achieve a reasonable muzzle velocity, but the weapon finally appeared in the early 1950s as the 'Skysweeper', firing at 45 rounds a minute.

The British development began in 1946 and was simply aimed at producing the best possible rate of fire from the existing 3.7 inch gun. The wartime guns, with time fuzes and mechanical rammers, had achieved 25 rounds a minute. Under the name 'Project Ratefixer' a number of feed systems were tried out in the late 1940s, and the result was 'Ratefixer CN' in which the gun was belt-fed, the belt being driven by an hydraulic motor. It achieved a rate of fire of 75 rounds a minute, a quite sensational figure which meant that no less than 2½ tons (2,125 kg) of ammunition was being shifted into the gun in every minute. But by 1949, when the project was completed, the 3.7 inch gun was feeling its age and it was thought advisable to develop a completely new gun. To make quite sure of success, two guns were projected; one was a taper-bore weapon, the calibre changing from 4.2 inches to 3.2 inches (107 mm to 81 mm), while the other was a smoothbore 5 inch (127 mm) firing a fin-stabilized projectile resembling the German Peenemunde Arrow Shell. The taper-bore gun proved too difficult and was scrapped; the 5

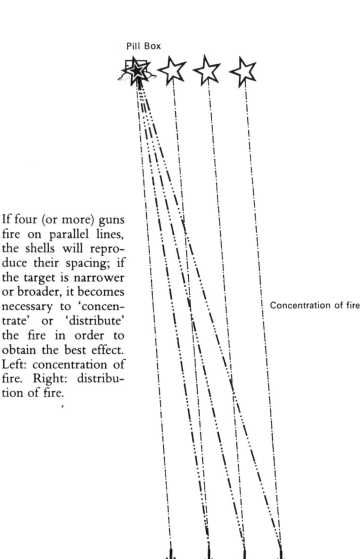

Pill Box

If four (or more) guns fire on parallel lines, the shells will reproduce their spacing; if the target is narrower or broader, it becomes necessary to 'concentrate' or 'distribute' the fire in order to obtain the best effect. Left: concentration of fire. Right: distribution of fire.

Concentration of fire

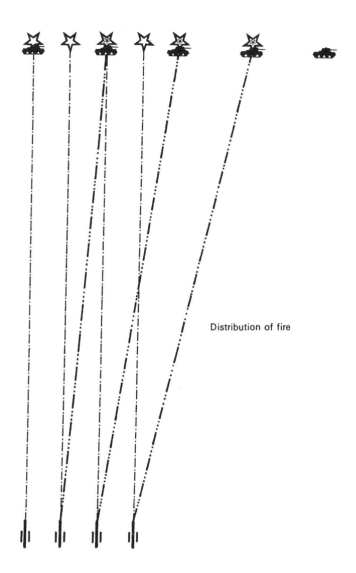

Distribution of fire

inch gun reached prototype form and turned out to be a 30-ton monster which would have taxed anyone's ingenuity to move it through an average urban area. Fortunately, before any further work could be decided upon, the first anti-aircraft guided missiles appeared, and in 1958 came the decision that 'no further attempts at a cannon solution for medium or heavy anti-aircraft defence' would be undertaken.

In the field artillery world, much of the postwar development was influenced by the nuclear threat, and several designs for self-propelled guns appeared in which the entire weapon and its crew were concealed behind armour so as to fend off fall-out, flash, blast and all the other dangers. But the same threat changed the nature of tactics in many ways, leading to the dispersal of forces all over the country instead of their concentration as in pre-nuclear days. The object in view, of course, was simply to prevent assembling sufficient troops in one place to make a nuclear strike worth the effort. This, in turn, led to some problems for the artillery; once upon a time an observer was sent to sit in a trench in the front line, from which, with the aid of nothing more sophisticated than a pair of binoculars, he could see what was going on across No Man's Land and call for appropriate action. But now, with this nuclear-induced dispersal of forces, he could sit there for days and see very little. What was needed was deeper observation, well into the enemy area; the Air Observation Post, which had performed so well during the war years, was now at considerable risk from missiles and well-directed light anti-aircraft fire, besides which it had never been the practice to fly AOP aircraft deep into enemy territory.

In the late 1950s, therefore, a new accent was placed on 'Locating', a broad-band expression which covered all the aspects of detecting targets. The old-style flash spotter was no longer of any use, since flashless and almost smokeless powders were now in use and in any case the ranges involved

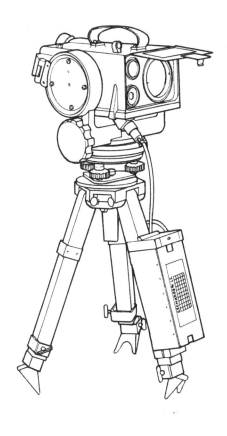

The most modern method of deter-
mining the range to a target is this
Simrad Laser rangefinder.

were too great for accurate spotting. Radar was brought into play, both for scanning the ground and for scanning the sky to pick up mortar bombs and gun shells in flight and, by applying computers to their track, calculate their origin and thus deduce the position of enemy weapons. Pilotless aircraft were brought in, mounting photographic cameras, television cameras, radar scanners and infra-red scanners, so that any selected area could be examined in detail by a remotely-controlled aerial sensor. Computers were brought into use to calculate gun data, take into account every possible variable, keep a running check upon gun wear, ammunition expenditure, calculate fresh data for targets held in memory banks, and, by means of data transmission links, make all this information instantly available to other artillery formations.

And if one side can do this, it is reasonable to suppose that so can the other, so in addition to building up its location ability, the modern artillery force has to take steps to avoid being located or, if that proves impossible, to mitigate the effects of being so spotted. And the best way to do this is to develop a 'shoot-and-scoot' technique in which extremely accurate fire (thanks to the locating services and the computers) is brought down very rapidly and then, before the enemy has had time to gather his wits and retaliate, the guns are moved rapidly away to some other location.

This immediately conjures up pictures of self-propelled guns, and this is indeed the way in which much artillery has gone. But there are other situations in which self-propelled guns are not the answer; the 'brush-fire' war in which victory goes to the side which can deploy moderate force very rapidly over a wide front or in rough country. And the answer to that is airpower, the ability to deploy troops by helicopter and aircraft. The average self-propelled gun is not air-portable, so that there is still space for the conventional towed gun.

In the 1950s the British Army were contemplating the adoption of a new field-piece, an 88 mm weapon which was essentially an improved 25 pounder. But before any decision could be taken, a NATO agreement was reached to the effect that the standard calibre for 'close support' guns – the new term for field or divisional artillery – would be 105 mm. No such calibre had ever existed in British service, and so it meant a completely new design had to be begun. The opportunity was taken to adopt a self-propelled equipment, which, in 1962, resulted in the appearance of the well-known 'Abbot' gun.

While this was being developed, as an *ad interim* measure a 105 mm weapon was needed, and an Italian design was selected. This was the 105 mm Pack Howitzer Model 56, developed by the OTO-Melara company. It was an ingenious design of a short-barrelled howitzer which had astutely been conceived to fire the standard American 105 mm M1 howitzer ammunition, of which there were vast stocks throughout the world, so that anyone purchasing the weapon would not be put to any difficulty in obtaining ammunition for it. It used a split-trail carriage and had the wheels mounted on pivoting stub-axles so that the height of the gun above the ground could be rapidly altered. With the wheels in the 'down' position, the gun sat well above the ground to give ample clearance behind the breech when firing at high angles; with the wheels swung 'up' the carriage lay close to the ground to give good stability when firing at low angles in the anti-tank role, for which both hollow-charge and squash-head ammunition were provided. As well as being adopted by Britain and other NATO countries, the 105 mm M56 was widely bought throughout the world. It is air-droppable, air-portable, can be slung beneath a helicopter, dismantled into twelve pack loads for carrying on muleback, towed behind a light vehicle such as a jeep or Land-Rover, or carried portée in the back of a three-ton truck.

When the British Army adopted the 'Abbot' SP gun, it also adopted a fresh design of 105 mm ammunition; the American design was, after all, some 30 years old by that time and modern technology offered more effective shells and longer ranges by using newer ammunition. Although the calibre was the same, the ammunition was not interchangeable with the American type used in the Pack Howitzer, which introduced an unwelcome logistic complication. Moreover, experience with the Pack Howitzer had revealed that it did not take kindly to long distance towing over rough country. In the late 1960s, therefore, a design of a new 105 mm towed gun was put in hand, a design which eventually came into service in the 1970s as the 'Light Gun L118'.

The Light Gun was designed from the outset to be as light as was compatible with ample range and performance. The Model 56 Pack Howitzer weighed 1,273 kg and had a maximum range of 10,575 metres; the Light Gun weighs 1,818 kg and has a maximum range of 17,000 metres firing the standard UK 105 mm ammunition. However, in order to cater for situations which might arise in areas of the world where ample stocks of the American M1 ammunition exist, the barrel of the Light Gun can be rapidly removed and a new barrel, chambered for the American shell and cartridge, be substituted; the weight remains almost the same, but the maximum range drops to about 13,000 metres.

The Light Gun, and the Pack Howitzer rely upon vehicles to move them; the Abbot drives off once its 'scoot-and-shoot' task is done. An alternative method of bestowing battlefield mobility upon a gun is to give it 'Auxiliary Propulsion', a technique first demonstrated by the Soviets in the 1950s when they revealed their 'SD-44' auxiliary-propelled 85 mm divisional gun. Basically, this was a conventional split-trail two-wheeled field gun; to this the Soviets added a two-cylinder petrol engine mounted on the left trail leg and driving the gun wheels via a short shaft. The trail ends were supported on a third wheel, which was steered by the driver, who sat on the trail leg in front of the engine, facing to the rear of the weapon. In this manner it formed a tricycle arrangement and could move over good country at 8–10 km/hr (6 mph) and on roads at 25 km/hr (15 mph). Thus, with this weapon it was no longer necessary to wait for the towing vehicle to appear; the gun could fire and within a minute could be packed up and rolling to a new concealed position, before retaliatory fire could be brought down on the position it had just vacated.

Auxiliary propulsion was tried on one or two other weapons, by both the Soviets and the Americans, using much the same system of simply strapping a motor-cycle engine on to an existing gun. On the latest weapon to be adopted by the British Army, though, the auxiliary propulsion system is an integral part of the design and, in fact, does more than merely shift the gun about.

After using various American self-propelled 155 mm howitzers during the late 1950s and 1960s, the British Army decided to ask for a more modern towed equipment with a better performance than could be obtained from the elderly American designs (for although the self-propelled chassis were new, the howitzer itself was of 1930s vintage). For various reasons, probably not unconnected with the vast expense of developing a new gun in these days, it became a joint venture between the British and German armies, and they were later joined by the Italians. The resulting weapon, known as the 155 mm FH70 (for 'Field Howitzer of the 1970s'), uses a split-trail carriage with a small platform which is dropped to the ground, and the wheels raised, for firing. In front of the wheels is the auxiliary propulsion module, containing a Volkswagen engine and a transmission unit to drive the main gun wheels. A two-wheeled bogie drops below the trail ends to support them when being driven by the A-P unit. In addition to providing movement, the A-P unit drives an hydraulic pump to provide power for opening and closing the trail legs, lifting and lowering the wheels and lowering the bogie wheels into place. For towing in the normal way, the drive can be disconnected and if, for any reason, the A-P unit is not functioning, then the hydraulic power can be provided by a hand pump.

The gun is conventional but uses modern ammunition to achieve a far better performance than any 155 mm howitzer of previous design. With a 43.5 kg (96 lb) high explosive shell it can range to 24,000 metres, and a proposed rocket-assisted shell is likely to improve this to 30,000 metres. The initial plans called for development of a fin-stabilized long-range projectile much on the lines of the Peenemunde Arrow Shell, but recent information is that this idea has been abandoned in favour of an American design of rocket-assisted shell.

A very similar weapon was developed by the Bofors company of Sweden under the title 'FH 77'. This has an A-P unit which in addition to providing movement also provides power for an automatic loading mechanism. This uses an hydraulic hoist to present the shell to the breech and a power rammer, and with it the howitzer can achieve a rate of fire of 15 rounds a minute. The A-P unit also provides power to elevate the gun, open and close the trail legs, lift and lower the recoil spades, lift and lower the trail when connecting to the towing vehicle, and, unusually, can be brought into action to drive the gun wheels when the equipment is being towed in difficult country, under full control of the towing vehicle driver. Unfortunately all this complication adds weight and cost, and it is not yet known whether the Swedish Army is prepared to approve the weapon for service.

*   *   *

Artillery has come a long way in the last sixty years. It has seen two types of cannon weapon come into and virtually go out of service – the anti-aircraft and anti-tank gun, both of which are now threatened by missiles in every level of employment. It has seen the absolute disappearance of heavy siege artillery, coastal defence artillery and horse-drawn artillery. But in spite of some pessimistic prophets – particularly in the 1930s when it was widely suggested that the field gun was now usurped by the tank and the heavy gun by the aeroplane bomb – artillery is still one of the most effective weapons of war. It is still one of the few weapons which can be used to advantage in any weather or condition of visibility, and the shell is one of the few potent weapons on today's battlefield which is immune to electronic countermeasure techniques. And even though the back-up is today highly dependent upon electronics and sophisticated instrumentation, the gun itself is still a robust and simple piece of equipment which rarely fails to work. About one hundred years ago a German, Prinz Kraft, wrote that the basic requirements of artillery were 'firstly that it should *hit*, second, *hit*, third, *hit*; and that it should be in the right place at the right time.' There seems little danger of that definition falling into disuse.

GLOSSARY

Autofrettage
A method of strengthening a gun barrel during manufacture by subjecting it to internal hydraulic pressure far greater than the firing pressure it will be expected to meet. Also known as 'Cold Working' in American terminology.

Bag Charge
A propelling charge for a gun or howitzer which is contained in cloth bags instead of in a metal cartridge case.

Barrage
System of artillery fire on which guns are laid so as to deliver a line of bursting shells in front of advancing infantry. The elevation is periodically changed so that the line of shells advances, protecting the infantry assault.

Base Ejection
Type of carrier shell (*qv*) in which the contents are ejected through the base of the shell at or close to the target. Used for smoke, gas, flare and leaflet-carrying shells.

Breech Ring
A reinforcing steel section around the breech end of the barrel, into which the breech closes.

Buffer
Method of absorbing the recoil of a gun; usually a cylinder full of oil, through which the recoiling gun draws a piston.

Calibre
The internal diameter of the gun barrel.

Carrier Shell
A shell (*qv*) which acts merely as a method of delivering a payload to the target, the shell itself having no designed tactical effect. The payload may be smoke, gas, leaflets etc.

Cartridge
The explosive charge which propels the projectile from the gun.

Concentration
Method of artillery fire in which the guns are laid so as to group the falling shells on one particular point for maximum effect.

Counter-Battery
Method of artillery fire against gun batteries of the opposing side.

Dial Sight
Optical gun sight in the form of a periscope with a head which can revolve 360 degrees and which is graduated so that the sight can be set at any measured angle. Used for indirect fire (*qv*).

Direct Fire
Artillery fire in which the target is in view from the gun, *eg* anti-tank fire.

Elevation
The angle between the horizontal plane and the gun barrel. For any particular combination of gun, projectile and charge there is a specific relationship between this angle and the range to which the shell will go. The maximum range of a gun is theoretically achieved at 45 degrees elevation, but in practice, owing to air resistance,

gravity and other considerations, it can be achieved at various angles up to 55 degrees.

Equilibrator	A spring or hydro-pneumatic device which balances the weight of the gun barrel so as to make the task of elevating it easier.

Geschoss	German: shell.

Geschütz	German term for gun; it implies a low-velocity weapon.

Gun	A piece of artillery which projects a shell at elevations less than 45 degrees and which uses a limited number of different propelling charges. Compared with a howitzer of similar calibre it will have a higher muzzle velocity and longer range.

Gunfire	Type of artillery fire in which the guns of the battery fire the specified number of rounds as fast as possible with accuracy but without reference to the other guns of the battery. *Cf:* Salvo (*qv*).

Haubitze	German: Howitzer.

Howitzer	A piece of artillery which can fire at angles above 45 degrees and which uses a number of various propelling charges to give a number of trajectory options so as to shoot over intervening terrain. Compared with a gun of similar calibre, a howitzer will have a lower muzzle velocity, will have a shorter range, and usually fires a heavier shell.

Hydro-Pneumatic	Operating by means of liquids and compressed air or gas; usually used in connection with recoil systems in which the buffer uses oil and the recuperator (*qv*) uses air or gas. Also used in connection with equilibrators (*qv*) using compressed gas and oil as a form of spring medium.

Hydro-Spring A type of recoil system in which the buffer uses oil and the recuperator is a powerful spring.

Indirect Fire Artillery fire in which the target is not in sight of the gun.

Jacket A short metal tube which supports the barrel of a gun and, sometimes, connects it to the recoil system.

Kanone German term meaning gun; implies a weapon of high velocity.

Monobloc A gun barrel forged from a single piece of steel.

Mortar Piece of artillery which is fired *only* at angles greater than 45 degrees. Nowadays usually used with reference to smooth-bore infantry weapons, but can refer to rifled artillery.

Muzzle Velocity Speed at which a projectile leaves the muzzle of a gun.

Obturation The sealing of the rear end of the gun (*ie* the breech) against the unwanted escape of gas from the propelling charge. In lighter weapons it is usually done by a metallic cartridge case, in bag charge guns by a resilient pad inside the breech mechanism.

Panoramic Sight American term for a dial sight (*qv*).

Recuperator Form of return mechanism which sends the gun barrel back into the firing position after it has recoiled. It

	may be a spring or a cylinder of compressed air or inert gas.
Salvo	Method of artillery fire in which all guns are fired at the same instant, thus ensuring that all the shells land together for maximum morale and shock effect.
Shell	Artillery projectile which is hollow; it may contain high explosive or some other tactical payload such as smoke or gas.
Shot	Artillery projectile which is solid and intended for penetration of armour or concrete.
Traverse	Horizontal movement of a gun in order to point it at the target.

APPENDIX 1

CONDENSED DATA TABLE FOR THE ILLUSTRATED WEAPONS

Plate No.	Title	Calibre inches	Weight in action	Elevation limits degrees	Shell weight lbs	Muzzle velocity ft/sec	Maximum range yards
1	British 13 pdr gun	3.0	2,236 lb	−5 to +16	13.0	1,700	5,900
2	French 75 mm M1897	2.95	2,510	−11 +17	16.0	1,740	7,500
3	British 120 mm MOBAT	4.7	1,685	−5 +30	28.3	1,515	1,000
4	British 3.7 in Pack How	3.7	1,856	−5 +40	20.0	973	6,000
5	British 4.5 in How	4.5	4,030	−5 +45	35.0	1,010	7,000
6	British 18 pdr Mk IV	3.3	3,507	−5 +37½	18.0	1,625	11,100
7	US 75 mm Gun M1917A1	2.95	2,990	−5 +16	15.0	1,900	8,865
8	Jap. 75 mm M38 (imp)	2.95	2,487	−8 +43	14.0	1,978	13,080
9	Jap. 70 mm Bn How	2.75	468	−4 +75	8.3	650	3,050
10	French 155 mm How M1917	6.1	7,275	0 +42	96.0	1,476	12,575
11	French 155 mm Gun GPF	6.1	23,700	0 +35	98.0	2,410	20,560
12	British 9.2 in How Mk 2	9.2	16.2 tons	−15 +50	290	1,600	13,935
13	British 60 pdr Mk 2	5.0	12,050	−4½ +35	60.0	2,125	16,400
14	British 3 in 20 cwt AA	3.0	6,000	−10 +90	16.5	2,000	15,700 feet
15	British 18 in Rail How	18.0	250 tons	0 +40	2,500	1,880	22,300
16	Italian 75/46 AA	2.95	7,395	0 +90	14.3	2,350	20,000 feet
17	Italian 149/40 M35	5.86	25,312	0 +45	112.0	2,620	24,000
18	French 105 mm M35	4.13	3,586	−6 +50	35.4	1,450	13,120
19	French Mtn 75 mm M28	2.95	1,455	−10 +40	16.0	1,230	9,846

Plate No.	Title	Calibre inches	Weight in action	Elevation limits degrees	Shell weight lbs	Muzzle velocity ft/sec	Maximum range yards*
20	Russian 76 mm M36	3.0	3,570	−5 +75	14.2	2,315	14,870
21	Russian 85 mm AA M39	3.35	9,470	−3 +82	20.2	2,625	24,000 feet
22	French Hotchkiss 25 mm AA	0.98	1,875	−5 +80	0.65	2,950	12,000 feet
23	Jap 75 mm Type 88 AA	2.95	5,380	−7 +85	14.4	2,360	21,200 feet
24	US 105 mm How M2A1	4.13	4,980	−4¾ +66½	33.0	1,550	12,205
25	German 105 mm leFH18	4.13	4,377	−6½ +40½	32.6	1,542	11,675
26	German 75 mm leIG 18	2.95	882	−10 +75	13.2	689	3,690
27	German 75 mm FK38	2.95	3,012	−5 +45	12.9	1,985	12,576
28	British 25 pdr Mk 2	3.45	3,968	−5 +40	25.0	1,700	13,400
29	French 155 mm How M50	6.1	18,075	−4 +69	96.5	2,125	19,410
30	Italian 47/32 M35	1.85	582	−15 +56	5.25	820	3,800
31	Bofors 40 mm L/60	1.51	4,368	−5 +90	2.0	2,700	5,000 feet
32	British 3.7 in AA Mk 2C	3.7	23,100	−5 +80	28.0	2,600	32,000 feet
33	German 88 mm Flak 36	3.46	10,990	−3 +85	20.8	2,690	26,250 feet
34	British 6 in 26 cwt How	6.0	9,262	0 +45	86.0	1,410	11,400
35	British 7.2 in How Mk 1	7.2	22,760	0 +45	200	1,700	16,900
36	German 105 mm LG42	4.13	1,191	−15 +42½	32.6	1,099	8,695
37	German FK 16nA	2.95	3,360	−9 +44	12.9	2,170	13,450
38	German s 10 cm K18	4.13	12,440	0 +48	33.4	2,740	20,860
39	German 17 cm K18	6.81	17.25 tons	0 +50	138.5	3,035	32,370
40	US 155 mm How M1	6.10	11,966	−2 +63	95.0	1,850	16,355
41	German 15 cm K39	5.87	26,900	−3 +46	94.8	2,838	27,010
42	Russian 152 mm How M43	5.98	7,938	−3 +63½	88.0	1,670	13,550
43	Russian 122 mm Gun M31	4.80	15,652	−4 +45	55.1	2,625	22,825
44	German 15 cm sIG33	5.91	3,749	0 +73	83.8	787	5,140
45	German 105 mm Flak 39	4.13	22,544	−3 +85	32.6	2,890	31,000 feet
46	German 75 mm Mtn 36	2.95	1,654	−2 +70	12.7	1,558	10,000
47	Jap. 47 mm Type 01 A/Tk	1.85	1,660	−11 +19	3.4	2,735	8,400

No.	Name							
48	Jap. 75 mm Mtn Type 34	2.95	1,180	−10	+45	14.0	1,265	8,750
49	British 2 pdr A/Tank	1.57	1,757	−13	+15	2.0	2,650	8,000
50	British 5.5 in Medium	5.5	13,646	−5	+45	100	1,675	16,200
51	British 17 pdr A/Tank	3.0	4,624	−6	+16½	17.0	2,900	10,000
52	US 75 mm Pack M8	2.95	1,339	−5	+45	14.0	1,250	9,610
53	US 37 mm A/Tk M3	1.45	912	−10	+15	1.92	2,900	12,850
54	US 3 in A/Tk M5	3.0	4,875	−5	+30	15.4	2,600	16,100
55	British 6 pdr A/Tank	2.24	2,521	−5	+15	6.0	2,693	5,500
56	US 90 mm AA gun M1	3.54	19,000	0	+80	23.4	2,700	33,800 feet
57	German 28 mm SPzB41	1.1–0.8	505	−5	+45	0.25	4,590	1,000
58	German 5 cm PAK38	1.97	2,175	−8	+27	5.0	2,700	2,900
59	German 75 mm PAK97/38	2.95	2,625	−8	+25	10.0	1,893	3,300
60	German 76.2 mm PAK36	3.0	3,815	−6	+25	16.6	2,426	9,840
61	German 88 mm PAK43	3.46	8,159	−8	+40	22.9	3,280	19,135
62	German 24 cm K3	9.44	54 tons	0	+56	334	3,183	41,000
63	Russian 100 mm M44	3.93	7,616	−2	+25	35.0	2,950	23,000
64	Russian 37 mm AA M39	1.45	4,410	−5	+85	1.61	2,885	14,000 feet
65	US 8 in How M1	8.0	14.15 tons	−2	+65	200	1,950	18,510
66	British 7.2 in How Mk 6	7.2	14.5 tons	−2	+63	200	1,925	19,600
67	German 75 mm FK 7M85	2.95	3,920	−5	+42	11.9	1,805	11,235
68	German 12.8 cm PAK44	5.03	10.0 tons	−8	+45	62.4	3,280	26,700
69	US 105 mm How M3	4.13	2,495	−9	+69	33.0	1,020	8,295
70	German 88 mm Flak 41	3.46	17,199	−3	+90	20.7	3,280	35,000 feet
71	German 88 mm PAK 43/41	3.46	9,658	−5	+38	22.9	3,280	19,135
72	German 17 cm K(E)	6.69	17.25 tons	0	+50	138	3,035	32,370
73	German 80 cm Gustav	31.5	1,329 tons	+10	+65	7.0 tons	2,330	23.61 miles
74	British Smith Gun	3.0	605	−10	+40	8.0	400	500
75	British Short 25 pdr	3.45	3,015	−5	+40	25.0	1,280	10,800
76	Italian 105 Pack M56	4.13	2,810	−7	+65	33.0	1,380	10,935
77	British 105 mm Light Gun	4.13	4,000	−5½	+70¼	35.4	2,325	18,590
78	US Vulcan M167 AA	0.78	3,000	−5	+85	0.25	3,570	3,200 feet
79	155 mm FH 70	6.1	19,400	−5	+70	96.0	2,715	26,245

APPENDIX 2

ANTI-TANK GUNS: COMPARISON OF PENETRATIVE PERFORMANCE

Note:

Penetration figures are based on performance against homogeneous armour plate, with the projectile striking on a line 30 degrees away from a line drawn perpendicular to the face of the target plate; this is an international standard which gives a measure of the shot's effectiveness when striking at an angle, since a 'perfect' side-on strike is highly unlikely to occur in war. Where figures are available, the comparison range is 1000 metres; in some cases, due to figures for this range not being available, the 500 metre value is shown. In general, these are for the smaller guns unlikely to be used at the longer range.

The type of projectile is indicated as follows:

APHE   A piercing shell containing a small charge of high explosive.
AP   A plain steel shot.
APC   Steel shot with a penetrative cap.
APCBC   Steel shot with penetrative and ballistic caps.
APCR   Armour piercing, Composite, Rigid; a shot containing a tungsten-carbide core.
APCNR   Armour piercing, Composite, Non-Rigid; similar to APCR but fired from taper-bore guns and thus is capable of decreasing in diameter to conform with the reducing calibre.
APDS   Armour piercing, Discarding Sabot; a multi-part projectile in which the lighter bore-diameter 'sabot' is discarded after shot ejection, leaving a tungsten-cored 'sub-projectile' to travel to the target and effect penetration.

Gun	Calibre	Type of Projectile	Weight of Projectile	Muzzle Velocity	Penetration
BRITAIN					
2 pounder	40 mm	AP	2.0 lbs	2,650	42 mm/1,000 m/30°
		APCNR	1.15 lbs	4,200	57 mm/1,000 m
6 pounder	57 mm	AP	6.25 lbs	2,693	74 mm/1,000 m
		APCBC	7.0 lbs	2,775	88 mm/1,000 m
		APCR	3.97 lbs	3,528	
		APDS	3.25 lbs	4,050	
17 pounder	76 mm	AP	17.0 lbs	2,900	136 mm/1,000 m
		APCBC	17.0 lbs	1,900	109 mm/1,000 m
		APDS	7.6 lbs	3,950	119 mm/1,000 m
					200 mm/1,000 m
USA					
37 mm M3	37 mm	APHE	1.92 lbs	2,650	30 mm/500 m
		APC	1.92 lbs	2,900	50 mm/500 m
57 mm M1	57 mm	AP	6.28 lbs	2,800	70 mm/1,000 m
		APCHE	7.27 lbs	2,700	70 mm/1,000 m
3 inch M5	76 mm	APHE	15.4 lbs	2,600	85 mm/1,000 m
90 mm Gun M1	90 mm	APHE	24.5 lbs	2,800	110 mm/1,000 m
ITALY					
47/32 Model 37	47 mm	AP	3.25 lbs	2,065	26 mm/1,000 m
90/53 AA Gun	90 mm	AP	22.5 lbs	2,755	101 mm/1,000 m
JAPAN					
37 mm Type 97	37 mm	APHE	1.48 lbs	2,500	35 mm/500 m
47 mm Type 01	47 mm	AP	3.08 lbs	2,700	40 mm/1,000 m
USSR					
45 mm M1937	45 mm	AP	3.4 lbs	2,500	38 mm/1,000 m

Gun	Caliber	Type	Projectile	Velocity	Penetration
45 mm M1942	45 mm	APHE	3.15 lbs	2,700	50 mm/500 m
		APCR	1.88 lbs	3,250	54 mm/500 m
57 mm M1943	57 mm	APHE	6.92 lbs	3,250	86 mm/500 m
		APCR	3.88 lbs	3,800	100 mm/500 m
100 mm M1944	100 mm	AP	34.6 lbs	2,950	186 mm/500 m
		APHE	34.4 lbs	2,950	153 mm/500 m
		APCR	20.7 lbs	3,600	181 mm/500 m
GERMANY					
2.8 cm SPzB41 (Taper)	28/20 mm	APCNR	4.6 oz	4,593	52 mm/500 m
3.7 cm PAK 36	37 mm	APHE	1.5 lbs	2,500	36 mm/500 m
		APCR	12.5 oz	3,380	40 mm/500 m
4.2 cm PJK41 (Taper)	42/29 mm	APCNR	11.8 oz	4,150	53 mm/1,000 m
5 cm PAK 38	50 mm	APHE	4.96 lbs	2,700	50 mm/1,000 m
		APCR	1.87 lbs	3,930	55 mm/1,000 m
7.5 cm PAK 40	75 mm	APHE	15.0 lbs	2,600	89 mm/1,000 m
		APCR	7.01 lbs	3,250	96 mm/1,000 m
7.5 cm PAK 41 (Taper)	75/55 mm	APCNR	5.71 lbs	3,690	145 mm/1,000 m
76.2 cm PAK 36(r)	76.2 mm	APHE	16.63 lbs	2,425	88 mm/1,000 m
		APCR	8.93 lbs	3,250	92 mm/1,000 m
8.8 cm PAK 43 & 43/41	88 mm	APHE	22.93 lbs	3,280	167 mm/1,000 m
		APCR	16.10 lbs	3,710	192 mm/1,000 m
12.8 cm PAK 44	128 mm	APHE	62.40 lbs	3,280	230 mm/1,000 m